Escape!!!

The True Story of a World War II P.O.W. The Germans Couldn't Hold

by John M. "Jack" Roberts

Escape!!!

The True Story of a World War II P.O.W.
The Germans Couldn't Hold

Non-fiction
by
John M. "Jack" Roberts

Published by

Brundage Publishing
203 Executive Office Building
33 West State Street
Binghamton, NY 13905

Jacket design by Barrie Hoople

Library of Congress
Control Number: 2003110382

ISBN Number: 1-892451-11-5

Printed in the United States of America

Foreword

Many people (including scholars, historians, veterans of war, and the media) have written stories about World War II. Their stories have covered numerous aspects of what happened including the horrors of the soldiers while fighting the war in the air, on land and at sea. Their stories range from the bravery of many heroes to the inhumane treatment of the prisoners of war.

I do not claim to be a hero of the war, nor do I possess historical facts about what happened in the various echelons of the United States Military Command and how they made decisions that led up to the many battles that raged. My intent is to tell a story about my personal experiences as a young man from Hamilton, Ohio who answered the call to duty and served his country faithfully and to the best of his ability as a soldier in the United States Army.

The story that I am about to tell has not been previously reported in detail. This book will join the archives of other stories written about personal wartime experiences. The information within these pages records how the war affected me as a young artillery soldier. No one knows my story like I do and no one else can tell it.

I can only assume that the reader understands what World War II was all about so I do not have to relate detailed facts about the conflict in Europe or in the South Pacific. The only details I will give will be those that affected my personal life in order to show the odds that were against the newly organized Division that I was with during the war. On December 10, 1944, within six days of arriving on the frontline in the Ardennes Forest on the German/Belgium border, the Division had its first taste of blood in battle. During the following six weeks the 106th Division fought a mighty enemy while at the same time enduring the harsh elements of the dead of winter.

My story will tell about individual heroism as I saw and it will show personal survival against all odds. My story tells what my buddies and I faced, what we went through to survive after being ambushed and captured by the Germans and how we were

able to escape our captors. None of our ordeal was without bloodshed, determination and faith in God.

To get a better understanding of the forces that the 106th Infantry Division faced on the morning of December 16, 1944 (when the Germans spearheaded through the Division and crushed the frontlines of the Americans) some facts must be made a part of this Foreword.

The Battle of the Bulge, as the German Counter-Offensive is titled, began on the morning of December 16, 1944 and ended on January 25, 1945. It was the coldest and snowiest weather experienced in the Ardennes within memory. Participating in this Battle were 500,000 Germans, 800,000 Americans and 55,000 British soldiers.

The German side had three Armies, and ten Corps, the equivalent of twenty-nine Divisions, in position. The Americans had three Armies, and six Corps, the equivalent of thirty-one Divisions. There was also the equivalent of three British Divisions as well as contingents of Belgian, Canadian and French troops, which eventually became part of the battle.

When the Battle of the Bulge ended, the Germans had suffered 100,000 casualties, including those killed, wounded and captured. The Americans suffered 81,000 casualties, including 23,554 captured and 19,000 killed while the British suffered 1,400 casualties including 200 killed. With the massive number of soldiers and armor in place for the German drive through the Allied Forces there was also a heavy loss of equipment on both sides. For example, each side lost about 800 tanks and the Germans lost 1,000 aircraft.

The 106th Infantry Division alone suffered 564 killed in action, 1,246 wounded and 7,001 missing in action by the end of the Offensive. Most of these casualties occurred within the first three days of battle when two of the Division's three infantry regiments were overrun, forced to surrender and taken prisoners of war.

Upon return to my unit I received promotion from Corporal to Staff Sergeant and I continued fighting in the war, later receiving a Battlefield Commission as a 2nd Lieutenant.

My military career ends in Linz, Austria following the end of the war, where I was assigned to occupational duty as a Military Government officer. I returned home in July 1946 at the age of 21, a little older and much wiser. How I met the challenges of once again becoming a civilian, finding a job, getting married and raising a great family are not included in this book.

In conclusion, I must say that I am proud to be an American citizen and that I was proud to be an American soldier and to wear the uniform of such a great country for three and one-half years. Furthermore, I put my life on the line to preserve the freedom that we so richly enjoy today so that future generations can live without oppression and raise their children in a free country. I can only ask succeeding generations to stand tall and be proud of the flag of the United States of America and to honor it, just as I have done, and as have all others who served their country, especially those who made the supreme sacrifice by giving their lives for their homeland. God Bless America!

John M. "Jack" Roberts
1st Lt. U.S. Army

This book is Dedicated to:

My wife Mary Louise (Staarman) Roberts, who tolerated me all of these years and who has given me two great sons of whom I am extremely proud; My eldest son Thomas David and his wife, my daughter-in-law, Juliana Mary (Bauer) and their children, my precious grandsons, Matthew Thomas and Michael Christopher and my adorable granddaughter Christina Julianne; My youngest son David Jonathan and his wife, my daughter-in-law, Susan Elaine (Dryden) and their children, another precious grandson Jonathan Richard and another adorable granddaughter Cecilia Marie.

And to all future great grandchildren that may be born of the union of my wife and me and to their mates and their families.

A belated dedication to my beloved parents, Robert Morton Roberts and Grace Josephine (Wolke) Roberts, who, under extremely trying circumstances, raised two sons and lived to see them grow up to become men and to take their place in the world. Their understanding and training set the foundation for my very existence and growth.

A special appreciation to my brother Robert John (Bob) Roberts, because life would not have been nearly as rewarding without him as a brother, playmate and friend. By being blood brothers, our relationship could not be faltered by anything throughout all the years that we were together. Even the many miles that eventually separated us were never at a disadvantage. We always knew that we were there for each other.

Credits

Credit for this book being written is affectionately given to my two sons, Thomas D. and David J. Roberts. Their sincere concern and encouragement to write about my interesting life in the form of an autobiography was the basis for the eventual writing of this book.

I permitted many people to read the chapters describing my life in the Army. They encouraged me to write a book that concentrated on my combat experience, but I declined to do it because I felt that that part of my life was past history.

A few years ago, I met a young retired Marine Staff Sergeant, Dieter Stenger, from Spotsylvania, VA, who heard about my story and asked to read those detailed chapters. After reading what I had been through, he became very excited and felt that my story should be written in book form. Again I refused the offer. In order to get me to do it, he offered to help me write the book, but again, I refused. However, he provided me with some factual data that he had researched for books he was writing about World War II. I accepted his help and encouragement to assume this difficult task. Frankly, had it not been for Dieter Stenger's encouragement, this book would not have been written.

The insignia of the 106th Infantry Division

Cpl. Jack Roberts
Ft. Jackson, South Carolina
July 1943

The Corporal stripes issued to
Cpl. Jack Roberts at Ft. Jackson, SC
July 1943

106th Infantry Division
592nd Field Artillery Battalion, Battery "C"
Fort Jackson, South Carolina
October 1943

First Row: **Jack Roberts**, Harry Hallberg, Dewell Mills, Earl Brown, Rodney Swing, Walter Grzybowski, Lt. Americo Spegarelli, Lt. Kincaid, Capt. Robert W. Smith (Battery "C" Commander), Lt. Vassichek, Lt. Walter Sohier, James Estes, Cpl. Hertk, Thomas Devoe, Ray Ostrowski, Frank Saramyzin
Second Row: Leonard Black, Louis Manzo, Millard Willis, Fred Dalessandro, Frank Kramer, Lionel Voisine, Elmer Martin, John Truglio, William Savage, Arthur Rychlowski, R. Hegman, Jimmy Leonardo, Tom Barbareti, Alfred Brondi, Delbert Walker, Leonard Livingston, Nathan Nickelson, James Jenkins, Walter Lego
Third Row: Ronald Davis, Michael Bertanzetti, Walter Boho, Bill Michie, Terrill Rigdon, Frank Costello, George Peterson, John Tuite, John Lundie, Sam Cohe, Jesse Wardlow, Albert Kirkland, John Hill, Albert Grimes, Bobbie Dokoupil, Robert Dillhoff, Sam Daskin, Pvt. Ortwine
Fourth Row: Leamor Alcorn, Peter Bourasaw, Michael Bakaj, Vince Desantes, David Cochems, Thomas Manager, Jerome Zelkin, Robert Costello, Edward Gopian, Aquila Nebeker, Ross Lawson, Aaron Hamblin, Robert Powers, Ray Rowland, John H. Jones, John Goliebiowski, Elwood Lorah, John Boberski
Fifth Row: Merle Ahlsen, Leonard Werner, Laurence Loudon, Earl Head, Frank Williamson, Kenneth Johnson, Walter Luckey, Sylvester Watkins, Delbert Wichtman, Gabriel Garguilo, Carl Himberg, Robert Floyd, William Witcher, Earl Jenkins
Sixth Row: William Henry, Bill Sewert, James Krysowski, Raymond Reese, Ivan Loukx, Hugh Williams, Virgil Williams, Harold Fossness, Brantley Howard, John A. Jones, Leo Cremer, Earl Winchester, Nick Caivano, Emil Hintze, Ken Arndt, Ernest Wendling
Seventh Row: William Addis, Earl Hudson, Earl Scheibly, Paul Carbaugh

Table of Contents

Chapter 1

My Family

I was born shortly after the end of WWI, "The war to end all wars." And I fought in WWII, which defeated three of the greatest tyrannies the world had ever seen: Germany Nazism, Russian Communism, and Japanese Imperialism.

Life started for me on Sunday, August 10, 1924 at 10:10 a.m.; I weighed nine pounds and six ounces and was born in Mercy Hospital in Hamilton, Ohio. I was the second son of Grace Josephine (Wolke) Roberts and Robert Morton Roberts. My brother, Robert John Roberts was born on July 6, 1922. My first name was given to me in honor of my grandfather, John B. Wolke, my mother's father. I was immediately nicknamed "Jack," just like my grandfather.

The first tragic event of my life happened when I was just four days old. My right arm was broken while I was still in the hospital. My mother told me that she thought the nurse dropped me. The nurses claimed that my mother laid on my arm while she had me in bed with her. I guess I will never know for sure.

At the time of my birth, our family lived on Elmo Avenue, in the Lindenwald section of Hamilton, Ohio. Mom and Dad rented a three-room apartment upstairs. The owners of the two-story frame house lived in three rooms downstairs.

My father was born on a farm in Jefferson County, Kentucky, near Louisville, on August 3, 1882. He was the youngest child of Albert and Catherine (Johnson) Roberts. Dad had six sisters and five brothers. My father's background was somewhat secretive. He spoke very little of his home life, and I always had a feeling that it was not very pleasant. He did, on rare occasions, speak about his youth, but being young I didn't pay much attention to what he was saying.

Dad told us that when he was entering his teens, the local country doctor asked him to become his trainee, to finish his education, and to enter the medical profession. Because of the economics of the farm, his parents refused to let him go because he and his brothers were needed to run the farm. In those days men practiced medicine without a medical degree.

Dad left home when he was twenty-one years of age, never to return or even to contact any member of his immediate family. Since he only had a fourth grade education, Dad confined his career to working as a "live-in" farm hand at various farms. His roaming took him throughout northern Kentucky and southern Ohio. When he settled down in Hamilton, he got a job driving a furniture truck for the Krebs Furniture Company. Although Dad had no formal education, he was an intelligent man. He could do most anything.

My mother was born on March 23, 1891 in Cincinnati, Ohio in the old German section of the city. She was the daughter of Mary (Abel) Wolke and John B. Wolke, both of German ancestry. Mom had four sisters and one brother. My grandfather Wolke, in addition to being a successful real-estate broker, owned a saloon called the "Sample Room", which he opened in 1892. My mother's family lived upstairs over the business.

Mom received a formal education up until the eighth grade. At a very young age, she and her sisters helped with the work around the saloon. Each daughter had her individual responsibility in helping to maintain the family business, such as cleaning, preparing the food, and washing the dishes.

Mom left home when she was twenty-five years old because her father was too demanding. She moved to Hamilton to live with her sister, Mae, who was married to Frank J. Burger. To pay her own way, Mom got a job as a stenographer at the Krebs Furniture Company. It was here where my mother and father met and began dating.

Mom and Dad were married on September 13, 1921 at St. Ann's Catholic Church in Hamilton. Dad, not being Catholic, agreed to take instructions in the Catholic faith and was converted and baptized just before they got married. Dad had no religion at all prior to converting.

Cramped conditions in the upstairs three-room apartment created the need for our family to seek larger quarters as well as a place where my brother and I could play. We then moved to a house on Clinton Avenue in Lindenwald. My father, with the arrival of his two robust sons, decided to quit his job at Kreb's Furniture and to buy a farm. Until he could get the farm profitable, Dad delivered milk for the Frechtling Dairy Company.

Back in those days not many people owned automobiles. A Ford automobile cost $290, which was expensive back then. But, right before we moved to the country my father bought a used Model T-Ford, which he would need for his new job. The Ford was an open "touring car." In the wintertime and on rainy days, you took the side curtains that came with the car and attached them to the outside of the car to keep the rain and the cold out. The car had no heater, so it was extremely cold on the inside. Mom kept big heavy blankets in the car so when we went someplace in the winter we would use the blankets to bundle up.

Later, Dad transferred to delivering ice cream in a truck from Hamilton to Cincinnati, Ohio. In fact, Dad became the first driver to make such deliveries. It only became possible to haul ice cream a long distance at that time, since dry ice was invented about 18 months earlier and was just now being marketed. Without refrigeration it was impossible to haul frozen products a long distance before that.

Chapter 2

Life on the Farm

The farmhouse, located near Mason, Ohio, was a large, two story, old stone house with an additional lower level where Mom did the laundry and where we ate some of our meals during the hot summer months. On the premises of the property was a large barn, smoke house, chicken house, spring house, pig pens, corn crib and a couple of other small outbuildings. We had horses, cows, chickens, ducks, geese, cats and always some breed of dog.

Since we had no refrigerator or icebox, the springhouse was our "ice box." All of our perishable goods were stored there on a shelf above the spring water, which flowed through the springhouse. Here is where we stored butter, eggs, and milk. It was cool inside and very damp since the springhouse sat back in the hillside and had thick stonewalls.

Life on the farm was not easy. It was especially hard for my mother who had never lived on a farm. Everything we did was hard work and there were no modern conveniences. I can never remember hearing my mother complain about anything. The main house had no plumbing or electricity. Water was obtained from a well just behind the main house. There was also an outhouse (a two holer) located behind the main house about fifty feet away. Toilet paper consisted of a Sears-Roebuck catalog or corncobs. We kept a "slop jar" under our bed for night use.

The only heat in the farmhouse was a large wood-burning stove in the kitchen, which acted as the principal heating unit for the house. The house, except for the kitchen, was very cold in the winter months. Mom had to do all of the laundry by using a washboard and tubs. I can remember her stooped over the hot tubs scrubbing the clothes on the board. Perspiration streamed down her face. Mom later got a hand-powered washing machine, which my brother, Bob, and I helped operate. The underside of the machine's tub was shaped like a half-moon and it fit inside a large wooden rocker that rotated back and forth as you pushed the handles. My brother and I would make believe we were on a railroad handcar as we pushed it back and forth.

When we first moved to the country, we did not have a telephone. Several months after moving there, we finally got one. It was a big wooden box that hung on the kitchen wall. You never answered the phone every time it rang, but only when your "ring" sounded. Everyone in the area was on a party line and the operator at a central control switchboard in Mason, Ohio, would ring the party that was being requested by a pre-assigned number of rings, such as 1-long and 2-short, or 3-long and 1-short, or 4-short and 1-long. Some of the local folks would listen in on other people's conversations just to be nosey.

My brother Bob and I were isolated out in the country. We had no other children to play with, except each other. The nearest children lived about two miles away, and we never even knew them. Bob and I were good friends and playmates. For fun, Bob and I would pull each other around in a wagon and pretend we were in a car, and also slide down the cellar steps on an old rug. We also made up imaginary playmates. Despite this, all was not play. As young as we were, Bob and I had our own daily chores.

Dad made us a sled from wood scraps. Bob, always full of clever ideas, decided we could get a better ride if we tied Corky, our German shepherd, to the sled. After we were both on, he threw our cat out front so that Corky would chase it. Corky's lunge sent Bob and me off the sled laughing.

During the summer months my father had steady work at the Frechtling Dairy delivering ice cream. He would get up early in the morning and he would not get home until late at night. Bob and I never got to see my father very much. I remember one time he came home while we were still up and I asked my mother who that man was. One of the reasons why I didn't recognize him was because he had shaved off his mustache.

Occasionally Dad had to go into town at night for a truck driver's union meeting. Once in a great while Mom and us boys would go along. The meeting for the drivers was held at the Anthony Wayne Hotel in Hamilton, and just across the street was the Rialto Theater. While Dad was in the meeting, Mom would take us to the movies. Most of the movies in those days were silent. However, in 1928 the first talking motion picture was created using a soundtrack that was actually on the film itself. The first talking film was titled *The Jazz Singer*, which starred Al Jolson.

The first movie I can ever remember seeing at the Rialto was a Charlie Chaplin silent film. One scene showed him hanging onto the front bumper of a car that was teetering on the edge of a cliff. I hid my eyes and screamed thinking he was going to fall off. My mother assured me that it would be all right, which it was. I went home that night and had a nightmare about the incident.

Since my brother, Bob, was two years older than I was, he went into the first grade following his sixth birthday. I really missed my playmate. I had to do a lot of make believing while he was at school and I always looked forward to him coming home in the afternoon. I would stand and wait for the school bus to drop him off at the end of the lane, which was some distance from our house.

The school he went to was in Westchester, Ohio, about six miles away from our house. I could not wait to go to school because I was so lonesome. I begged my mother to let me go. One day, she finally gave in. In order to enroll me, my mother had to lie about my age. She told the school officials that I was six when I was really five years old so that I could enter the first grade.

Chapter 3

The Great Depression

1929 was a disastrous year. The farm did not pan out well for my folks. The country experienced one of the worst droughts that summer. The crop yield was practically nothing. Without the crop yield, my folks could not make the payments on the farm. We had a hired hand who worked the farm for room and board. Dad's job could not support the family and keep up the farm. The farm had to be self-sustaining to survive.

We had enough to eat because Mom was able to can the things that grew in the garden. We also had a few trees that bore fruit that she stored in jars and butchering took place in the fall.

That same year, the country entered an economic disaster. The Roberts family became one of its many victims. The stock market crashed and banks started failing. Just before the crash, in October of 1929, the Stock Market was a bull market that was out of control. The crash of the market and bank failings were the start of the Great Depression, which lasted several years and caused many people to lose their savings, their homes, and their investments.

Since Mom and Dad could not make the payments on the farm, the City Loan Company, who loaned the money to my parents to buy the farm, foreclosed on the mortgage. We lost our farm, the equipment and the livestock. The only items that we salvaged were the furniture, our clothes, our foodstuff, and our Model-T Ford. For the next ten years, Mom and Dad made monthly payments to the City Loan in order to pay off the farm property that they no longer owned.

I had just started the second grade in 1930 at Westchester School when we moved off the farm and back to Hamilton. I would continue the second grade at St. Ann's in Hamilton. My folks found a two-story house to rent on Brough Avenue in Lindenwald for $25 per month. The school year had already begun when we enrolled at St. Ann's Catholic School. Being taught by Catholic Nuns was certainly a new experience.

Bob and I felt a little strange living in town. It certainly was not like the farm. In some ways we liked it better because there were more kids to play with in the neighborhood and we had far less chores to do.

Bob and I made many friends with the kids in the neighborhood. We never parted as playmates, even though other kids entered our lives. We grew close by living on the farm. However, we began to form our own groups of friends.

When I was six years old, I got an opportunity to sell magazines. The magazine was called the "Delineator." I can remember when I came home and told my parents that I was going to sell magazines from door to door. They couldn't believe it. They thought I was too young, but I was persistent and won out. I guess they admired my early ambition to help supplement the family income.

Dad traded in his Model-T Ford for a used 1928 Chevrolet. It was a much warmer car in the winter months because it was a closed sedan without side curtains. Though only one or two days a week, we were always grateful that Dad had work. People were feeling the crunch of the Depression. Many were without jobs. Of the 122,775,000 people in the United States, 4.5 million were unemployed.

My folks were having a rough time financially and decided that the Brough Avenue rent was too expensive. They just couldn't afford it along with the payments on the farm foreclosure. In order to save money, when Bob or I had a hole in the sole of our shoe Mom would cut a piece of cardboard and fit it inside the shoe to keep the cold air out and to keep from wearing holes in our socks. Thanks to some of our relatives for the "hand-me-down" clothes.

We then moved to St. Clair Avenue, which was only four blocks away. It rented for $20 a month, which was $5 less than the Brough Avenue property. This gave us $5 more for other living expenses.

Six months barely passed when the owner of the St. Clair Avenue property decided to put the house on the market to sell. Once again, we had to look for a different place to live. This would be the third move in less than two years.

In 1931, I completed the third grade. Bob was detained in the fourth grade at St. Ann's. That put Bob and I together in the same grade from then on. Bob and I sure hated to move. We liked the city, the neighborhood, the school, and our friends.

Mom and Dad found a place on Dixie Highway, in Butler County, a small mini-farm that had about ten acres of ground. We rented the property from a family by the name of Betz. The rent was $2 cheaper per month than the St. Clair property. In addition to the lower rent, the folks were attracted to the country setting of the Dixie Highway property. They thought it would be nice for us boys to live in the country again. There were also several fruit trees on the property and land for us to grow our vegetables. Since the Depression was still in full force, growing our own food helped save money.

After moving, Bob and I were enrolled at Stockton School, which was an old, two-room red brick schoolhouse with four grades and a wood-burning stove in each classroom. After our first summer on Dixie Highway, we entered the fifth grade. Since there were no school buses, Bob and I walked two miles each way to school, rain, snow or shine. A male teacher taught the upper four grades and he was very strict. In those days, it was an accepted practice for a teacher to spank, and even hit, the pupils if they felt that the student did something wrong.

One day Bob did something that our teacher didn't like. He took a swing at Bob with his fist but as Bob tried to duck, the teacher's fist hit Bob squarely on the nose and blood squirted all over the school room, which caused him to be frightened. He took Bob out into the cloakroom where the well water pump was located and tried to get Bob's nose to stop bleeding. It took a long time, but it finally stopped.

When Bob and I got home from school that evening, Mom took one look at Bob's bloody clothing and asked what happened. After we explained the incident, she cleaned him up, changed his clothes and told us not to tell Dad. We couldn't tell Dad because he believed that the teacher was always right. If Bob did something that caused the teacher to strike him, then Bob would get another whipping at home because Dad was a physical disciplinarian.

America's economic system began to show some signs of improvement. When many of the unemployed returned to work on the various Government projects, their purchasing power also increased and more expendable goods were being purchased. Also, Henry Ford restored the $5 per day minimum wage to 47,000 workers. All of these things had an effect on the ice cream business, which increased consumption dramatically and gave Dad extra days of work each week.

One day the owners of our rental home told us that they wanted to return to their own home because the owner was recalled to his job as a Coremaker in Cincinnati. That meant that we had to move again—it seemed like we were always moving. Just as soon as we got used to one place, made friends, and got used to the school, we had to start all over again.

From the Betz house, we moved to Hanover Township, which lay west, in the opposite portion of Butler County. We attended the Hanover Township School, which was about six miles from our house, so we rode the bus.

The dwelling was a four-room bungalow. Bob and I slept in our double bed in the unfinished attic, which had no insulation and very little air circulation. It was very cold sleeping in the winter, and on hot summer nights we slept on the floor downstairs. However, listening to the rain on the roof on rainy nights was delightful. While living here, Dad returned to work full time, so our parents bought a second-hand 1935 Plymouth automobile.

My first romantic kiss was one of my fondest memories while living in that house. It happened while a group of neighborhood boys and girls were playing hide-and-go-seek. For some reason, the neighbor girl from across the road decided to hide in the same place that I had chosen. She was a pretty young girl with dark hair and brown eyes. We kind of liked each other, and in those cramped quarters we looked deep into each other's eyes and I gave into my impulse to kiss her sweet, soft lips. What a thrill it was. Having been sought and found, my love life abruptly ended.

My brother and I planted and tended a garden behind our house; we were members of the school's 4-H Club. While living in the country, we learned a lot about farming and gardening. Because of those experiences, we were selected to make a presentation during the Annual County Fair at the Butler County Fair Grounds in Hamilton, Ohio. Using charts and a pointer stick, we described our products from the time of planting to harvesting. Unfortunately, we did not win a prize.

Our family moved two more times. The next move was to a home in Lindenwald at 720 Chase Avenue—a neighborhood where the other houses were nicer than ours was. The four-room bungalow used a wood-burning "pot-bellied" stove to heat the entire house consisting of a kitchen, living room, and two small bedrooms. A hand pump in the kitchen alcove drew water from the well, and there was no bathroom. Since we didn't have any plumbing, we had the only house in the neighborhood that had a "two holer" in the back yard, and where the neighbors could watch us coming and going. Mother did the laundry in a washtub in the kitchen. We also used the tub for bathing.

Bob and I returned to St. Ann's Catholic school at the start of the school year, where we both entered the seventh grade. Four months later we moved again, which was the last time we moved as a family. From birth through grade school, we ended up living in nine different homes and went to seven schools by the time we graduated from high school.

Upon entering the seventh grade I learned something quite unique. Our first day in school the nun took roll call. As our names were called we were instructed to answer "Here, sister!" When I heard the name "John Roberts" called I did not reply. I casually looked around the classroom to see who would answer because some kid in the room had a name similar to my name. When the name "John Roberts" was called a second time I still did not answer. The teacher approached my desk and asked me, "Why didn't you answer when I called you name?" I said, "Sister, my name is 'Jack Roberts.'" She said, "No, your name is 'John Roberts.'"

After school I went home and asked my mother what my name was. She looked at me kind of puzzled and said, "Jack Roberts, why do you ask?" I then told her the story about what happened at school. She laughed and that is when I first learned that I was baptized with the name of "John," which was my legal name, and that I was named after my grandfather "John" Wolke and was nicknamed "Jack." That cleared up the mystery.

Chapter 4

A Permanent Home

In January 1936 we moved into a rental house on Hamilton's West Side. The house had five rooms: a living room, dining room, kitchen, two bedrooms, and a bathroom. We finally got rid of the outhouse. The basement had a low ceiling, which made it necessary to duck your head. There was a coal-fired furnace and a coal bin in the basement. This house became our permanent home.

Changing schools in the middle of the year was always tough, but this would be the last time, other than High School. Bob and I enrolled at St. Peter In Chains Catholic School.

There were a lot of kids in the neighborhood for Bob and I to become friends with. We began to go our own ways and started to establish our own friends and develop our own interests. I became a boyhood pal with Dick Zihlman, one of my neighbors. We found things to do that were interesting to the both of us. Occasionally we would walk to town on Saturday to go to the movies. Going to the movies in those days meant that you would see a double feature, a newsreel and a cartoon all for the price of one admission of ten cents.

Never in our growing years did Mom and Dad give us an allowance. First of all, they never had the money and secondly, they felt that if we wanted anything over and above our food and clothing, then we should earn our own money. Mom and Dad continued to pay off the farm loan in addition to paying the rent.

In order for us to have our own spending money, we found our own jobs. I ran errands such as going to the corner grocery store for the neighbors. They usually tipped me a nickel or a dime. My source of income was mainly from the neighbors for cutting grass in the summer or shoveling snow in the winter.

We always made our own snow shovel by sawing a few boards and nailing them together. All of my grass cutting jobs were in the immediate neighborhood. I charged fifty cents a lawn and furnished my own mower. The customer would occasionally give me an extra nickel or dime if the grass were exceptionally long.

In May of 1937, Bob and I graduated from St. Peter's School's eighth grade class. Grandma Wolke came up from Cincinnati, Ohio for the graduation Mass at St. Peter's. For graduation Mom and Dad bought me a brand new bicycle and Bob got a dress suit. At the time of graduation I was twelve years old and Bob was 14.

Soon after graduation, Bob got a part time job working as a clerk at the City Market grocery store. Dad had taught Bob how to drive when he was thirteen because he thought someone else in the family besides Mom should know how to drive an automobile in case of an emergency. Like Bob, I wanted to drive, too. I was certain that I was old enough, but my parents kept putting it off. At age thirteen, Mom finally gave in. She took me to a gravel road out in the country and let me drive the car. What a thrill! I obtained my driver's license at age fourteen.

We did not have a telephone. If we needed to make a call our neighbors who had a telephone would allow us to use it. Later, in our freshman year in High School, Bob and I convinced our parents that we should have a telephone. What a great luxury that was.

Chapter 5

The Radio and World News

In 1937 we bought a new radio for the living room. The radio we had was one that Grandma Wolke gave us and it didn't work half the time. The radio Mom and Dad bought was a table model set in a wooden shell. It was the latest thing on the market because it had "push buttons". They were pre-set for the five radio stations in Cincinnati: WKRC, WLW, WSAI, WCPO and WCKY. The sixth button was the on and off button. We really wondered what we had. I can remember bringing my friends in the house to show them our new "Push Button" radio.

Radio was a wonderful invention. That year we were able to hear the first Atlantic to Pacific radio program by Herbert Morrison, broadcasting the landing and subsequent explosion of the German dirigible, the "Hindenberg," at Lakehurst, New Jersey on May 6th. What an ungodly event and emotional eyewitness reporting by the newscaster. Just six days later, we were also able to hear the first worldwide radio broadcast in the United States of the Coronation of King George I of England.

Also in 1937, there was a lot of conversation along with many newspaper articles being written about what was happening in Europe and the Far East. Adolf Hitler, the Dictator of Germany, was building up his armed forces and putting a lot of pressure on the neighboring countries for concessions. Some countries had already been invaded. The Japanese were flexing their muscles in the Far East and they were at odds with the Chinese. Most people in the United States wanted to ignore what was going on in the troubled world.

The politicians in Washington kept informing the people that foreign affairs cannot be ignored and what was happening on the other side of the world could become a real threat to the United States. One of the first encounters the United States had with reality was on December 22, 1937 when Japanese planes sank the United States Gunboat "Penny" while on patrol in

Chinese waters. I could not imagine at the time how these events would later affect my whole life.

Chapter 6

High School, Jobs, Girls

On August 10, 1937 I turned thirteen years of age. The last week in August my brother Bob and I registered at Hamilton Catholic High School for our freshman year.

Hamilton Catholic High School was an all-boys' school and was operated by the Society of Jesus, a religious order of young men who dedicated their lives to teaching. We addressed these young men as "Brother." When conducting class, the Brothers wore a black suit, black tie, and white shirt and they always wore a coat in the classroom no matter how hot it was. The suit coat had a long tail extending to the backs of their knees, better known as a "Prince Albert" coat. There was also a priest on the teaching staff who was of a different order. The Brothers and the priest lived next door to the private school in a large three-story house.

There was also an all girl Catholic school located in the second ward of Hamilton, Ohio that was operated by the sisters of Notre Dame and appropriately called Notre Dame High.

Young enough to relate to the teenagers, but old enough to have respect for the students, the Brothers were a great bunch of guys with high morals. Most of the Brothers were in their late twenties, or very early thirties. The Brothers set a fine example for maturity and manhood. I am grateful for the Catholic education and background that I received from Hamilton Catholic High. In addition, I am forever grateful to the parishioners of St. Peter's Church, our parish church, who paid the tuition, which made it possible for me to attend this private institution. These were the impressionable years. Discipline in high school came through punishment. Instead of physical punishment the students either lost privileges or were made to do extra homework.

Located across the street from Hamilton Catholic High was Hamilton High School, the public school for both boys and girls. At least we got to see the opposite sex once in a while. To keep us from looking out the windows at the girls, our school had the blinds mounted upside down on the windows and were pulled half way up. Enough light came in to see but our view of the girls and the outside was blocked out.

I tried to be involved in high school activities. I worked on the scrap paper drives each year after school and I sold raffle tickets for festivities held on the school grounds. In my freshman year I performed in the school's minstrel show. In my junior year, I took part in my school minstrel as a chorus singer.

Between my freshman and sophomore years I got a job as an usher at the Rialto Theater—the same theater in downtown Hamilton where I saw my very first silent movie as a child. My job at the Rialto Theater took up most of my after-school time, so I never participated in sports programs. Since Bob and I had to earn our own spending money, I was more interested in making a buck than getting involved in the various school activities. Many of our classmates received an allowance from their parents and usually they were the ones involved in most of the school functions including sports.

During my sophomore year, I continued almost the same schedule at the Rialto, except that I had to go into work just as soon as I got out of school in the afternoon. I was soon promoted from usher to the "Ticket Taker" and my pay was raised from $1.50 to $2.50 per week. This job was a perfect job for me because I could also do my school homework when business was slow.

The theater box office closed around 9 p.m. when the last movie started. The cashier took the cash receipts for the day to the second floor where she and the Manager prepared the bank deposit. The money had to be deposited nightly in the night bank vault at the First National Bank about two blocks away. If the manager or the cashier could not go or did not want to go to the bank, I would be asked to make the deposit. I was given the key for the bank vault and the feeling of importance came when I was escorted to the bank by a Police Officer. In those days the police walked a beat in downtown Hamilton. We really never worried about being robbed or mugged in those days. Policemen were friendly and most people respected their position of responsibility to the city and its residents.

I always tried to catch the last bus home, which stopped in front of the theater at 11:10 p.m. If I missed the bus I had to walk three miles home. Sometimes, if the movie was long, I would automatically miss the bus. If I had to walk from the theater at night, I wouldn't get home until after midnight and then I had to get up at 6 a.m. in order to walk to school. This pace began to affect my health after awhile and I eventually suffered the consequences.

I met a lot of girls while working at the theater. One in particular was a girl by the name of Ruth Stuart. I dated her casually for a couple of years. She and her sister came to the show every Saturday night. She was a pretty girl with long blonde hair and always returned my smile when she handed me her ticket. After the movie was over and as she left the theater she always smiled when she walked out. Then when she waited for the bus in front of the theater I could see her looking my way. I started speaking to her when she came in and from then on we became friendly. One time when she came in to the movie she invited me to accompany her on a "Weenie Roast" with a group of her friends. This started our casual dating. She was a real nice kid. As a matter of fact, I ended up taking her to my Senior Prom in 1941.

In the spring of 1939 a big event happened in our family. The owners of the house we were renting approached Mom and Dad and asked them if they wanted to buy the house. When my folks figured out their budget they decided to make an offer, which was accepted. Also, since all of us liked the house and the neighborhood, making an offer was only logical. Besides, we would not have to move anymore.

In my youth I met another good friend, Bill Webster. Bill was my age and also went to my high school. He was a year behind me in school but I was a year ahead of my age group. Bill and I started to chum around together and soon after Dick Zihlman became a part of our group. Bill was quite handsome, and a charmer. All the girls liked him. I met a lot of girls through him. We never seemed to get serious with the girls we met, but we had fun. Dick Zihlman found a girl in Lindenwald and started to date her more frequently.

As I grew older, I developed different interests. I began to pay more attention to the music world. I couldn't play an instrument, but I did like to listen to music. I bought records every so often. I bought "The Beer Barrel Polka," "Elmer's Tunes," "Pennsylvania Six Five Thousand," "Chattanooga Choo Choo" and a few other tunes that were popular then. I remember my mother holding her ears when I played some of the songs on the wind-up "Victrola" and she would say, "How can you stand that racket?"

My junior year was the year that we had to decide what kind of a career we wanted to follow. We had two choices: commercial or academic. There was no doubt in my mind as to what I wanted to do. I knew that I wanted to work in an office in the business world. We were told that if we wanted to go to college we should take the academic courses, such as physics and chemistry, because those courses would be required for fields such as medicine and engineering.

I continued to work at the Rialto Theatre. I was promoted to "Head Usher" and my responsibilities and hours were increased along with my pay. I would now be making $5 a week. I was responsible for all of the floor ushers and the ticket taker. I found the increased hours to be a little more than I could handle, but I kept at it. I was too proud to admit that I could not handle both school and work. I was just not getting enough rest and I was tired all of the time.

I started to lose weight and I became quite ill and confined to bed. Mom called our family physician and he came to our house to examine me. He sent me to Mercy Hospital for a chest x-ray. It was determined that I had a case of pneumonia and I had a spot on my lung. When my doctor found out that I was going to school and working full time, he told me that I had to quit one or the other. I could not continue to do both and stay healthy. The obvious choice was for me to stay in school.

I missed a total of fifteen days of school from the last part of November 1939 to the first part of December. I called the Rialto Theatre manager and told him of my illness and said that I would not be returning to work. He was sympathetic and agreed that I should finish my schooling.

A few days later, on December 12, 1939, a tragedy fell upon our family. I had just returned to school from being ill when Bob and I were called out of class. It was early that morning and our first class had just started when we were called to the Principal's office. He told us that our mother called and that we had to go home right away. Bob and I ran to Fifth and High Streets and got on the bus and headed for home.

When we got home, Mom was crying and there was a man at the house from the Frechtling Dairy along with the Hamilton Police Department, who had already told her the terrible news. The information they gave us was very sketchy and all we were told was that when Dad was delivering ice cream to Mark's Pharmacy he had been shot in the chest by a robber who was in the process of "holding up" the drug store on Reading Road in Cincinnati.

The man from Frechtling Dairy wanted to take us to General Hospital in Cincinnati. Mom decided that since I had been so ill and just returned to school, I would be better off to stay home. Just she and Robert would go to the hospital. They went to the garage and got Dad's car and Bob drove it to the hospital so they would have a way back home.

I stayed home that day and heard no word from anyone until Bob and Mom finally got home very late that night. The long hours and the anticipation I spent waiting on some kind of word were endless. All I could think about was the resentment I had for the bandit who shot my father. I felt robbed, cheated, and frustrated.

Mom and Bob arrived at General Hospital when Dad was still in the recovery room. The surgeon told Mom that they cut Dad's chest wide open and examined all of his internal organs and then could only say that it was a miracle that he was not killed instantly. The bullet had entered Dad's chest and missed his heart by about one-quarter of an inch, grazed his intestines, nipped his liver, grazed his stomach and then lodged in the muscles of his back. Because of the severe loss of blood, Dad had to have a blood transfusion.

The surgeon told Mom that it was also a miracle that the bullet did not do even further damage and that Dad would be on the critical list for a while. Their concern was that infection could set in because of the dirty bullet going through his body and the fact that he had to be opened up so wide and have all his internal organs moved around while the doctors looked for any damage. I attribute the miracle of his survival again to the good Lord. The good Lord saw fit to continue my father's life so he could be with his family for a while longer.

There were many articles written about the shooting in the *Hamilton Journal News*. Bob Crow, the reporter who covered the story, was a neighbor and he took a personal interest in the story. Cincinnati newspapers called to publish the story, and to ask for an interview and photographs of Dad. Mom kept a scrapbook about the shooting. The last news article appeared on July 20, 1940 regarding the conviction of the three bandits who held up the pharmacy.

Dad did not receive his weekly wages from Frechtling Dairy while he was absent from work. Instead, the State of Ohio paid him Workman's Compensation, which was less money than he would have made on the job. Frechtling Dairy felt no responsibility for the shooting, but his boss was compassionate throughout the ordeal. Dad returned to work in April 1940, four months after the incident.

While going to high school Mom would occasionally ask Bob and me to stop at the Elite Bakery in downtown Hamilton to pick up a loaf of homemade bread, rolls, or a cake on our way home from school. Another bakery that we stopped at on the way home was McGregor's Bakery on Main Street. In the rear portion of the Elite Bakery sales area was a small section of booths and tables where the customers could sit and enjoy a Coke, a sandwich, baked goods, or ice cream while listening to the juke box. This was *the* place to go because it was where many of the teenagers hung out.

Mom and Dad never permitted us to "dilly-dally" after school. We were supposed to come right home after school and get our lessons before we went outside to play. Besides, we didn't have money enough to visit or to hang out every afternoon like some kids did.

Saturday nights were fun nights. Dick Zihlman, Bill Webster and I would walk to town. This was the only night that we went to the Elite Bakery. The place was always crowded and we had to stand and wait before being seated. A fountain Coke cost five cents, so that is what we ordered. Then we sat there sipping, talking, and watching the girls. If we stayed too long, the management would ask us to leave if we weren't ordering anything else. No one ever got mad. We respected the request and just left.

Downtown Hamilton was always crowded on a Saturday night. People came to town to window shop or to go to the movies. The boys came to town to see the girls and the girls came to see the boys. In those days, none of the stores were open for business after 6 p.m.

At the end of May, Bob and I saw our junior year completed. Since I quit the Rialto and was now spending full time on my studies, I raised my grade average from the year before. The summer of 1940 was to be our last summer as high school students. Next summer we would be graduates and out on our own in the real world.

The day after Labor Day of 1940, Bob and I returned to Hamilton Catholic High for our senior year. Having just turned 16 years old, I would graduate as the youngest member of the Class of '41.

Mom and Dad were very pleased that Bob and I completed high school and received our diploma. I think that since Mom and Dad had no formal schooling, they could see that if Dad received a better education might have held a better job and could have provided more for his family. Dad always told us that we should keep our grades up and finish high school. He also used to say, "Don't end up as a truck driver, like me!"

Mom always seemed interested in what we did. I always considered her inquisition to mean that she was truly interested in our lives. Perhaps she was just being nosey. Of course, like most children, we only told Mom what we wanted her to know. There were times that I told Mom things that must have been boring to her, but she always acted interested. I communicated better with my mother than with my father. Dad never really seemed too interested when I tried to tell him things. In many cases he would find fault with what I did, and I guess I got turned off. I used Mom as my sounding board and to seek advice. A child needs at least one parent to communicate with. Mom happened to be that parent for me.

Meanwhile, in the foreign news, the situation in Germany was not getting any better. Adolf Hitler was making all kinds of promises and threats to neighboring countries. He ended up invading them regardless of what he said. His military was getting stronger and it looked as if he not only wanted to take over all of Europe, but also take over the entire world. He had already invaded Poland and Yugoslavia, he was at war with Russia and he was threatening France and England. The United States knew it was only a matter of time before they became involved somehow.

On September 16, 1940, Congress enacted the first peacetime selective service draft for the Armed Forces. It was planned that 900,000 young men would be taken each year. Those who could register were men between the ages of twenty and thirty-six. Camps for training created more jobs and added to the economy of the country. In fact it was on November 30th that the Willys Company, an automobile manufacturing company, made the first Jeep, which was tested at Camp Halabid near Baltimore, Maryland for use by the military.

The world situation was beginning to hit home with the drafting of our young men. It was called a peacetime draft, but everyone had a gut feeling that it was an undeclared wartime draft. As time passed, more and more of our friends and neighbors were being called to duty. Since I just turned sixteen years old at the time, four years seemed like a long way off before I would face being drafted.

Mom enjoyed family life and she liked to see everyone in the family get along. She did not tolerate bickering or backbiting. Bob and I had a good relationship with Mom and Dad, in spite of Dad's excessive whippings. He was a stern disciplinarian. Up to the time we became teenagers, he used a leather strap to whip us when he thought we did something wrong. Many times we had welts on our back, butt and legs.

To my knowledge, drugs weren't being used in our High School. Perhaps our temptations were minimal compared with the youth of today. However, I do believe that even if they were available, we would never have gotten into them. Mom instilled in us that we should never do anything that would bring shame to our family. That statement covered a lot of territory.

The same held true for sex. Like all boys, sex was discussed, but there was never any open sex. If it happened it was by a few kids and it was not bragged about. Mom told us to respect girls, treat them like ladies, and do nothing to offend them. Promiscuity was unheard of in our circle of friends. Heavy necking and petting was as far as it went, but no sex. My Catholic education also had a lot to do with my behavior.

More and more young men were being drafted. There were two ways of knowing the extent of the draft. Firstly, the draftees' names were published in the *Hamilton Journal News* every time a group was inducted. Secondly, the patriotic and popular thing to do when a member of the family went into the Armed Services was to hang a small banner in the window of the home of the person in the service. The banner was 9" x 12," with a blue outer border and a blue star set in a white background.

As one walked the streets and looked at the private homes, more and more blue "stars" began to appear in the windows. Later, during the war, if the star was gold instead of blue, it meant that a military person from that home had been killed while serving his or her country.

Our senior prom took place on May 24, 1941. It was held at the Gibson Hotel in Cincinnati, Ohio. The prom was to be a dinner/dance. My date was Ruth Stuart, the girl I had been dating on occasions since our meeting at the Rialto Theater. Bob's date was Ann Conjuga, who was from New Miami, Ohio. Bob and I decided to double date, and for transportation, we asked our parents to use the family car, our 1935 Plymouth.

Dad was a bit reluctant at first, but he finally agreed to let us take the car to Cincinnati. He gave us a long list of restrictions that we had to meet. We agreed that Bob would be the driver. We also agreed that we would not take anyone else with us in the car, we wouldn't speed or horse around, we would be careful, we would not drink too much alcohol and we would not get home too late.

Since Ruth Stuart went to Hamilton High, none of the guys in my class saw her before. Most of the other guys' dates were from Notre Dame Academy, the all girl Catholic High School. That evening, Ruth and I walked hand in hand into the Gibson Hotel's Italian Room, where we were to eat dinner before we danced. She was a knock out. My classmates stood there with their mouths wide open. Ruth wore a full-length red velvet evening dress. It was strapless and form fitting. Her peachy white shoulders surrounded by the long blonde hair made her look like a model. Ruth also had a great body. I was really proud to have her as my date that night, and the guys swarmed around her like flies to honey. They all wanted to know who she was and where on earth did I ever find her. We had a great time at the dinner and while dancing.

Mom had asked me not to get too serious with Ruth because of our age. Shortly after the prom, we drifted apart.

Ten days after the prom, on June 3, 1941, our commencement exercises were held in the auditorium of Hamilton High School, across the street from our high school. Family and friends were invited to the exercises. We wore a black cap and gown for the ceremonies. The evening was quite impressive and I enjoyed it very much.

For graduation, Mom and Dad gave us each a Waltham wristwatch as a present. My buddy Dick Zihlman received a used 1936 Plymouth from his parents. I was glad to see Dick get the car because I knew that we would be going places together when he was not with his girlfriend.

My school days were now over. I had managed to maintain a B+ average throughout my senior year. Graduation was a somber time. I looked at it with mixed emotions. Here I was, on one hand, a grown man entering the world and on the other hand, I was just a young boy of sixteen, a kid at heart looking forward to a long life ahead.

My concerns about the future were not groundless. The fear of war was the talk behind closed doors, and open in barbershops, saloons, and at the work place. The newspapers were printing more and more about the ravages of war in Europe and the rumblings in Japan.

Chapter 7

War Clouds and One Last Fling

Graduating from high school now meant that Bob and I must look for full-time employment. I knew that I did not want to work in a factory. Bob was hired as a machinist in a plant making "war" material. I wanted to work in an office. When I discussed looking for a job, my mother instructed me to make sure that I presented a good appearance. She made certain that I wore my best suit and shined shoes. She told me, "A first impression is a lasting impression." She also coached me to use my best personality and to be polite to whomever I talked to in an interview.

The day after graduation, I went job hunting. I applied for work at several factories for a clerical job. When I applied and listed my age as sixteen, I was given the brush off. Some said that I had to be eighteen, which was not true because work permits could be obtained at my age from the City of Hamilton. Others said that there were no openings in my line of work. I felt that I was being rejected based on my potential draft status. At one place, the employment manager was honest enough to tell me that my age prevented me from being hired.

I struggled to get a job. Within two days, I applied to work at fifteen retail stores. I finally got a job at Keiser Clothing Company. It was unexpected because when I first applied for a job at Keiser's and spoke to the manager he abruptly told me that they were not hiring. I never left an application or my name or telephone number. I never even knew the name of the person I spoke with. I must say I did make a nice appearance when I was job hunting. I was very neat, courteous, and friendly.

After arriving home from the job hunt, I received a telephone call from Keiser's. At first I could not understand how they knew how to locate me. It so happened that there was a man working there who lived on our street. Concluding that there had been some talk after I left Keiser's, our neighbor must have identified me to the manager. I was really fortunate that he was there. I returned to the store and was hired as a clerk where I sold men's apparel, except suits, topcoats and shoes.

Keiser Clothing was a prestigious, two-story men's clothing store. The prices were slightly higher than at other clothing stores but the merchandise was good quality. I was extremely proud to get the job and looked forward to working there.

When I told my parents I was hired, my mother was the only one who was excited. Dad was not as excited as Mom. He said that I should find a job with an organization that had possibilities for promotion. Of course he was right, but at the time I could not see it. I was just happy to have a full-time job.

I worked forty-nine hours a week for $10. The fellow I was assigned to work with and from whom I was to learn the business was Eugene Epperson nicknamed "Eppy." Eppy, a graduate from Hamilton High, was in charge of a small department. Eppy and I became the best of friends during the time I worked there. Eppy was extremely intelligent and a regular guy. He eventually joined with my group of friends and we ran around together.

Bill Webster and I spent a lot of time together on weekends since neither of us was dating steady. Since neither of us owned an automobile, we took rides in his father's car, walked to town or went to the Malt shops to listen to the jukebox and dance with the girls.

I will never forget the day that Bill and I were playing cards at his house on Eaton Avenue. It was Sunday December 7, 1941. We listened to music on the radio while we played cards. A voice interrupted the music and announced that Japan had made a surprise bombing attack on the United States Naval Station at Pearl Harbor in Honolulu, Hawaii. The first report was that damage and loss of lives were high.

Bill and I just looked at each other. We stopped playing cards and started talking seriously about what the incident meant to our country and what it could mean to us as individuals. We were the same age. I was seventeen at that time and the draft age was twenty. Being drafted in peacetime was one thing, but being drafted during a time of war meant that there was a good chance that we may be faced with a combat assignment and see action.

Bill and I had a good idea that war would now be declared with Japan. The radio stations all switched to their newsrooms and tricd to give the public as much information as was available. I left Bill's house and walked the long walk home. I had plenty of time to think about the prospect of a dismal future.

President Roosevelt called Congress together and declared a formal state of war against Japan. This turn of events was rather frustrating because the American public figured that if we were to enter a war it would be in Europe with Germany. Just two months before the attack on Pearl Harbor, a German submarine sank the US Destroyer, the Ruben James.

When I got home, Mom and Dad were listening to the radio also. We talked more about what the Pearl Harbor attack meant to all of us, especially for Bob and me. We continued to listen to the news on the radio. The public was later advised that the sneak attack on Pearl Harbor cost the US the loss of the battleships: Arizona, California, Alabama and Utah, while five other battleships were damaged extensively. Four destroyers also sank. By the time the attack was over 3,000 American lives were lost. The Japanese lost 28 planes and 3 midget submarines.

Four days later Germany and Italy declared war on the United States, and Congress adopted a resolution recognizing a state of war with both countries. Now we had a war going on each side of the globe. This was a very depressing time for all Americans.

After the formal declarations of war by Congress, the whole country began to change its attitude about what was going on in the world. Before that, many people wanted to believe that the problems were *over there* and that it couldn't happen here. The population was finally hit with reality. Everything that could be converted to war work began to happen. Food processing plants began to make more food and rations available for the Armed Services, which would create shortages at home.

On December 22, 1941 Wake Island was invaded and fell to the Japanese. Five days later the Office of Price Administration (OPA) announced that automobile tires would be rationed. This started a series of other items that would be rationed to the public.

On January 1, 1942 the automobile companies stopped making cars in their plants and began to build airplanes, Jeeps, trucks, tanks, guns, ammunition and other items for the war. In Vancouver, industrialist Henry J. Keiser produced the first 10,500-ton Liberty ship in a record four days.

In the spring, Congress announced that the draft age was being lowered from twenty to eighteen years of age. My being drafted was getting much closer. I was seventeen and my brother Bob was now nineteen. He now had to register for the draft. I knew that I would have to register on August 10th.

More and more of our friends, neighbors, and relatives were enlisting. The draft was expedited and more young men were being drafted into various branches of the Armed Forces. The entire country was starting to feel the pinch that goes with war. The conversation among people we met was always about the war and about the boys in the service. Rationing was taking on additional items. Used and scrap metal was vital. The population was requested to turn in anything made of metal that could be used in the war effort for making guns, trucks, ships, etc. The cities replaced their streetcars with buses and were digging up their old streetcar tracks and turning them in for scrap metal.

Women were going crazy because they could no longer get all the silk or nylon stockings they wanted. Whenever a store would get a few pair in, the word spread like wildfire. The girls that worked in offices in downtown Hamilton would leave their job just to get a pair or two. Silk and nylon was important to the Armed Forces because the materials were desperately needed for making parachutes and other items.

While working at Keiser's in the summer of 1942 they hired a new young girl to work behind the desk to wrap the sold merchandise and take the cash for articles sold by the salesmen. After making my first sale of the day, I went to the wrapping desk as usual and the regular desk clerk introduced me to the new girl. Her name was Mary Lou Staarmann. I had heard of her before because a classmate of mine at Hamilton Catholic was dating her. I thought she was kind of cute and very pleasant. We kidded around a lot.

In the meantime my buddy, Bill Webster, began dating a girl who worked as a soda fountain clerk at McGreevy's Ice Cream Store in Lindenwald. One day Bill had his father's car and we stopped in to see his girlfriend and get an ice cream cone. It was close to her quitting time so we stayed there so Bill could take her home. When we arrived at her house, I went in with Bill and was introduced to her parents and her two sisters, Anne and Patty. The instant I met Anne, I knew I was in love. She was a very pretty blonde girl with blue eyes. She was also Catholic, a rule that Mom laid down if we ever wanted to go steady with a girl. Bill said later that she liked me. I asked Anne for a date and from then on we began to go steady. Unfortunately, without my own car, I had to rely on my friends for transportation or take the city bus.

Anne's parents really liked me. It wasn't long before her parents and my parents became the best of friends and played cards at each other's houses. In fact, her parents thought that some day Anne and I would get married.

During the next several months Anne and I had a lot of fun together. She liked to smooch a lot, so I was in seventh heaven. Annie liked to tap dance and was rather good at it. I would attend the various local shows she performed in. She really had a great looking pair of legs.

Anne and I became very close. I found myself spending a lot of time at her house. They had a player piano in the living room and a lot of young people came to the house because of the three girls. Many evenings we sat around in the living room singing songs while someone pumped the piano. Anne's father liked his beer. He also liked to sing even though he could not sing very well. He liked to sing all of the old WWI songs because he served during the First World War. The days when I did not see Anne, I ran around with my buddies.

On August 10th, my eighteenth birthday, I had to register for the draft. The rules were that you had ten days to register after becoming eighteen. I registered at the Selective Service Board located in our downtown Post Office.

In October, my co-worker and friend Eugene Epperson was drafted into the Army. All of his co-workers at Keiser had a going away party for him at a private camp out in the country. I borrowed Dad's car for transportation to the camp. We all had a great time at the party. Around the time it was over, I asked the new girl, Mary Lou Staarmann, if she needed a ride home. She said one of the other salesmen brought her, but if I wanted to take her home she would go with me.

Mary Lou and I left the party and on the way home I pulled to the side of the road and we just sat there and talked for a while. It wasn't long before I decided to kiss her. She responded eagerly. What the heck, we were both young and she was kind of cute. What I didn't know was, Mary Lou was engaged to a former classmate of mine at the time and he was in the service. We had a pleasant evening, but we never went on a date together again. We got along very well together at the store, and it was just a casual relationship.

Before 1942 ended, coffee was added to the list of items to be rationed. Also, the factories were looking for people to fill the defense jobs because of the increased workload since the young men were leaving for the service. Congress abolished the WPA work program enacted during the Great Depression. For the first time many factories, in order to get an adequate supply of manpower to fill its needs, were forced to hire women in the shop areas on jobs that were traditionally considered to be just for men, like welding, press operators, truck drivers, machine operators, laborers, etc.

1943 arrived and it brought my brother Bob and me closer to the reality of being drafted. Sure enough, Bob received his notice to report for his physical on February 5, 1943. After his pre-physical he was officially drafted at the Armory in Cincinnati, Ohio. Back then when the draftees were inducted at the Induction Center in Cincinnati they were given the option of entering either the Navy or the Army. Bob chose the Navy. Being a skilled machinist, he thought that he could follow his work skills on board a ship. On February 12th he reported for duty and was sent to Great Lakes Naval Training Station in Chicago, Illinois.

Chapter 8

Into the Army

On February 3, 1943 I received a post card notice form the Selective Service Board stating that I was being summoned to take a preliminary physical for possible induction into the Armed Services. I reported to Mercy Hospital on February 4th. Ten days later I received an official "Order to Report for Induction," advising me to report to the Federal Building in Hamilton at 8 a.m. on March 1st. I arrived at the Post Office at the appointed time along with several other men where we boarded a bus and were taken to the Armory in Cincinnati, Ohio for a final physical. We were told that if we passed the physical and written tests we would be inducted into the Army or Navy.

The Armory was like a mad house. There were men from all over the tri-state area taking physicals, written tests, and walking from one station to another in all stages of dress or undress. When I completed all of the requirements my name was called and I approached the front where there were representatives from the Army and Navy seated at a table. I was asked what branch of service I wanted to serve in. I knew I wanted the Army, and said so. One of the main reasons I chose the Army was because I did not know how to swim. I wondered what I would do if I got assigned to a ship and the ship got hit. Sometimes I wish I could have taken back my choice. Bob told me that in addition to following his trade in the Navy, he always had good food and a nice place to sleep with clean sheets. I think he made a wise decision.

Upon leaving the Armory, we were instructed to return home and that in the next seven days we should wind up any personal affairs we might have before reporting for active duty. Our group was also informed that when we reported for active duty, we were to bring nothing with us except a safety razor, shaving cream, toothbrush, toothpaste and a comb. The government would furnish everything else.

When I arrived home that evening I told Mom and Dad about my experience in the Armory. The next day I went to Keiser's to inform my boss John Ruewe that I had been accepted in the Army and that I could no longer work there. The only personal affairs that I had to take care of were saying goodbye to my family and friends.

Most of our friends in our age group were being drafted or they were enlisting. About the time I was drafted, Dick Zihlman joined the Marine Corps. Shortly after I was inducted, Bill Webster joined the Navy. The general mood of the population was quite patriotic, and the guys who were not called into the service began to feel uneasy about it. In fact, some parents of the boys in the service were known to make nasty remarks to young men just walking the streets. I know it had to be true because when I was working at Keiser's and waiting on customers, some demanded to know why I was not in the service. I excused them because I knew how they must have felt about their own sons being in the Service.

I spent most of my seven days with Anne. She promised to write to me every day and said she would be looking forward to me coming home. The day before I left for the Army was very sad for the both of us. She gave me another one of her pictures and made me promise to miss her every minute.

March 8th arrived. Mom came to my room that morning to wake me, but I was already up. I did not sleep well that night. I put my personal belongings in a paper bag and Mom and Dad drove me to the Post Office. The other fellows who were going to the Induction Center also assembled. Sgt. Schulteiss, the Army Sergeant assigned to our group, told us to walk to the B&O train depot and board the train to the Induction Center. Mom and Dad drove to the train station to bid me farewell. About forty of us walked the half-mile to the station. Fortunately, it was a pleasant day. When the conductor called "All Aboard," I hugged and kissed my Mother goodbye. She was crying. I wanted my Father to hug me, but instead he shook my hand. The train pulled out and we were off to Fort Thomas, Kentucky for further assignment.

When we arrived at Fort Thomas, the first thing we did was go to the supply depot to receive our uniform and other items along with a cardboard box. After that, we marched to our assigned barracks, had our bunk assigned and were then told we were to change into our Army uniform and put all of our civilian clothes in the paper box, seal it up and label it to be sent home. We were then taken to the Army Post Office where we turned in our box for shipment.

We then went to lunch (called chow in the Army). After chow we were given our identification (dog tags). They were two identical tags with our name, serial number, blood type and religion. Mine read, "John M. Roberts 35791572," "O" (my blood type), "C" (representing my religion as being Catholic). Both tags were worn around the neck on a chain or cord. The idea of two identical tags is when a soldier is killed in battle, one tag stays on the body and the other is placed on the grave.

The barracks at Fort Thomas were two-story brick buildings on the outskirts of the city. It was used as a base camp for inductees and was similar to those used during WWI. There were several such buildings, with a mess hall, a library, officers quarters, administrative offices, a post office, and a building that housed a USO center where the soldiers could go to write letters, get a free cup of coffee and a doughnut or read magazines. In the evenings the USO offered entertainment.

After changing into our uniforms, we found that not too many of us got a very good fit. We were issued one set consisting of underwear, a dress blouse (jacket), shirt, trousers, hat, overcoat, high top shoes, and a barracks bag (to carry clothing and belongings); all khaki in color. We were also issued a "mess" kit with eating utensils. I must admit that I was proud to be a soldier and to wear the uniform of the United States Army.

Next, the barracks Corporal showed us how to make a bed "Army style." This meant that the sheets had to be stretched tight and the blanket had to be tucked in so tight that not a wrinkle could show. To make sure the bed was made properly the Corporal took a fifty-cent piece and dropped it on the bed. If the coin bounced, the bed was made properly. I was so naïve that I thought I was not allowed to pull the covers loose from the sides. The first night I slept on my back all night because the blanket fit so tight it kept me from turning over and I hardly slept. The next day I learned differently.

Outside we marched directly to the barbershop on site. We were lined up and there were several barbers cutting hair. As soon as one soldier got out of the chair another got in. In less than five minutes a hair cut was completed. A lot of waves hit the floor that day, including mine. This was called a GI haircut, which left very little hair on your head.

My pay as a Private was $50 a month. We could keep it all or we could sign up to have some of it sent home. I chose to have most of mine sent home because I knew that Mom and Dad could use the money.

There is no privacy in the Army. I learned this on the very first day. Everything was out in the open—showers, urinals, toilets, beds, meals, etc.

The second day, after evening chow at the mess hall, I walked over to the USO center for something to do. There were small rooms for reading and writing letters along with one large room where the entertainment was held. I walked into the large room where I heard a band playing. The band was seated on a small stage where they faced the audience. I found an empty seat and sat down to listen to the music. After each song, the bandleader played any requests that the soldier had. If the band could not play the requested song, the soldier would receive a pack of cigarettes. I began to think about songs that may stump the band.

After listening to a few songs, I happened to think about a song that my brother Bob sang as a solo in our first Minstrel show at Hamilton Catholic High School. The song "Longing" was written by a former graduate of the school who had it copyrighted, which made it a legitimate song. When I requested the song, the bandleader just stood there and looked at me. He then turned to the band and all the guys just looked at each other and shrugged their shoulders. The leader turned to me and said, "Soldier, if you can sing that song for us, you win." I sang the song for him. When I finished singing the song, everybody applauded and the leader handed me a pack of Lucky Strike cigarettes. It felt good to be a winner.

The Fort Thomas Induction Center was a busy place with new recruits coming and going. On March 13th I was one of the many recruits to receive the word that we were being shipped out the next day. We were not told where we were being sent. I called Mom and Dad and told them that I was leaving and I would write them as soon as I reached my destination. I asked them to call Anne and tell her of my departure.

Many of us were loaded on a bus and taken to a train sitting on a siding nearby. There were several passenger cars filled with soldiers. We were told which car to board as a group. None of these rail cars were sleeper cars so we were required to sleep sitting in our seats during travel. We began a long ride and only received two meals each day. We had to get in a long line at chow time to get to the "mess" car at mealtime and had to take our "mess kit" with us back to our seats while the train was swaying without spilling the contents. Then after chow we had to return to the mess car to wash our mess kits and utensils.

Three days later, on March 16, 1943, several cars from the troop train were dropped off at a siding at Fort Jackson in South Carolina. I was thrilled to be there. I had never been so far away from home and I was impressed with the outlay of the camp. What a new and exciting experience this was for me.

When we arrived at Fort Jackson, an Army Officer welcomed us and told us that we were being assigned to the 106th Infantry Division, a new Division just being organized. I was assigned to Battery C, 592nd Field Artillery Battalion. On March 15, 1943 the 106th Division was formally activated at Fort Jackson but actually came in existence on November 29, 1942 by War Department authorization. It was one of the 100 newly authorized Divisions which was to go overseas following a training more rigorous and more thorough than ever given to American troops before going into battle. The theory was that each new division would begin as a homogenous group with recruits brought in around a hardcore group called a cadre from already trained units.

The training laid down by Army Ground Forces stated that each Division would be progressive and balanced and coordinated from the beginning. The end result was that each Division, when moved to the battlefront, would be a team with its officers and men knowing one another as well as their skills. The only thing lacking would be the first thirty minutes of combat, the vital "kill or be killed" moment which only comes with battle.

I was one of the original soldiers of the new Division. The hardcore cadre units came from the 80th Infantry Division. Originally, the 106th Division was one in which the stress for enlisted personnel was on youth. The average age of the division when it was organized was twenty-two years of age.

When the 106th was finally built to full strength, it numbered 12,533 enlisted men and 708 officers. Our Battery Commander was Captain Robert W. Smith, from Greenwood, Indiana. He was small in stature, but tough and intelligent. He was a "true blue soldier" and took his commission as an officer quite seriously. Besides being tough, he was fair. Captain Smith ran a good battery. He was a good leader and commander, but he rarely smiled.

Early on I discovered that there were a lot of nice guys in my unit, and some not so nice. You quickly learn how to pick and choose your friends. Three guys that I teamed up with, and became very good friends, were Bill Sewert from Lewisburg, Ohio, Carl Himberg from West Roxbury, Massachusetts, and Ernest Tippet, from Bridgeport, Connecticut.

After dismounting from the train, we were taken by truck to our Battery site. We then received our barracks assignment in Battery C, and went to the Supply Room to draw supplies such as sheets, pillowcases, fatigue uniforms, leggings, and helmet liners. Two barracks buildings housed C Battery personnel; I was assigned to the second floor of building No. 1. We were told to turn in our soiled clothing to the supply room every Monday morning right after chow. For this purpose, we were issued a barracks bag that had our name and serial number stenciled on it. We also turned in our sheets and pillowcase at the same time. When turning in our laundry, we had to make out a laundry ticket listing the items in the bag. On Thursday we picked up our clean laundry at the supply room. Quite often, something was missing or you received items that belonged to someone else and were usually the wrong size. Many of us thought the reason this happened was because the laundry was washed and packaged by Italian prisoners of war at the POW (Prisoner of War) camp at Fort Jackson. They probably did it out of spite.

Fort Jackson had dry cleaning shops and barbershops located in the same buildings as the Post Exchange (PX) throughout the camp. We had our haircut often because it had to be kept short at all times. It took less than five minutes to get a hair cut and cost twenty-five cents. Also on the post were theatres that played the latest movies at a cost of ten cents.

Shortly after the 106th Division was organized, each unit was issued a pennant called a "guidon." The guidon for each Field Artillery Battery was a red flag mounted at the top end of a long pole. In the center of the pennant was a set of gold-colored crossed muzzles of two artillery cannons. Also in gold, above the cannons, were the numbers 592 representing our battalion. Beneath the cannons was the letter "C," denoting our battery. During battery marches the soldier who was in the lead carried the guidon.

Each day began with a wake-up call at 5 a.m., roll call at 5:30 a.m., and chow at 6 a.m. At 7 a.m. we "fell out" into formation as a group outside the barracks where we lined up in formation and received our orders for the day and to where we were to report. From there we marched to the parade grounds for calisthenics exercises and close order drill. Afterwards, we marched to various classes. During the workday, we always marched no matter where we went. Each day's activity was posted on a bulletin board outside the First Sergeant's office.

Over the next few weeks, we had learned the complete nomenclature of artillery warfare. We were also subjected to barracks inspections, barracks detail (work), and health classes included venereal diseases and an orientation on what was happening in the European and Pacific wars.

Our weekly orientation class was held on different days throughout the week, sometimes it was held on Saturday afternoon right after lunch. These classes were held in various buildings or out in the open, weather permitting. We were brought up to date on the trends of fighting in Europe and in the Pacific and were advised of enemy strength, as well as our own, various battles and their frontline demarcations, and casualties. Marked-up large maps were always displayed. When movies of the fighting were available the session was held in one of the theaters. The films were not newsreels but actual movies of various battles taken by Army or Navy personnel. Many of the orientation presentations were gruesome. The Army held nothing back. We were shown bloody fighting, therefore, we all knew what to expect when we got into battle overseas.

Within the next couple of weeks we were given our Section job (MOS) assignments. There were cannoneers, the soldiers who worked at the gun site, gunner Corporals; radio operators; linemen, those who laid the telephone lines and operated the field telephones; truck and Jeep drivers; and motor maintenance. My assignment in the Detail Section was that of a Scout Corporal, not in rank, but in title only. I would have to earn the rank later on.

The insignia of the 106th, which became official on May 1, 1943, was the head of a lion in gold (representing strength and power). The background was blue, which stood for the Infantry. At the circular border was a red circle, which represented the artillery support. Each soldier wore the insignia (shoulder patch) on his left arm near the shoulder. We were required to sew on our own patches. Each division had its own unique patches.

Each morning we continued with our calisthenics and precision drill exercises. It was tough, but I really liked doing it. I tried very hard to be a good soldier and to get along with my leaders and fellow soldiers. I learned that it paid off. Since the battery was in short supply of non-commissioned officers, they started to make *Acting Corporals* to help with the leadership assignments.

One day at reveille, my name was called to report to the Captain's office right after chow. I thought, *Now what did I do?* I could hardly eat breakfast. After breakfast I reported to the First Sergeant's office. No one ever saw Captain Smith without first going through First Sergeant Lewis. When you entered the

Captain's office, it was military procedure to walk up to his desk, snap to attention and salute him.

Sgt. Lewis announced to the Captain that I had arrived and we were invited in. I snapped to attention and saluted. The Captain said, "At ease, soldier." He then told me that the Sergeants had been watching me during training and I had responded very well. He then told me he was making me an "Acting Corporal." I could have died I was so thrilled. This meant that I was an acting non-commissioned officer and I would have all the authority of a Corporal but without the true rank or raise in pay. We were being tested. The Captain then handed me a blue band with two red vertical stripes on it to be worn on my left upper arm as my identification and authority for issuing orders.

With the new acting rank, I was in charge of taking groups of my fellow soldiers on the drill field each morning to put them through the paces of close order drill and calisthenics. In effect I was their drill sergeant. I was also put in charge of the second floor of our barracks. My responsibility was to make sure the area was clean and orderly at all times. Here is where I first learned that to get the maximum cooperation from people you ask rather than order them to do things. I also worked side by side with them in the barracks. I had no problems with the guys. I was truly a proud soldier. There were several other acting corporals made about the same time within our battery.

Periodically, we had inspections of the barracks and I always wanted to be sure that my floor passed the inspection. Sometimes they were surprise inspections, but most of the time they were announced ahead of time. The place had to be spotless and some of the guys were born slobs. They took a little extra attention.

On inspection, the Battery commander came through the barracks usually accompanied by one of his senior officers, a Major or Colonel. The floor had to be spotless, the beds had to be perfectly made, the shoes under the bed had to be shined, and our foot and wall lockers had to be open with everything arranged neatly therein. We were allowed one photograph over our bunk on a shelf, or on top of our locker. Most of the guys had a picture of either their girlfriend or wife. The guys who had pictures of naked women attached inside their lockers had to hide them during inspection. Sometimes they got caught during a surprise inspection. The inspecting officer ordered them to be removed with a slight grin on his face.

As noted earlier, at 5:30 a.m. roll call we had to be dressed in fatigues, shaved, and ready for duty. The late sleepers barely made it, some half-dressed and some never made it at all. Sometimes a buddy would holler "Here" at roll call to cover for him.

We always had a big breakfast at our mess hall. A hearty breakfast consisted of hot cereal, bacon and eggs, bread, jam, butter, and coffee. Sometimes we had cold cereal, hot cakes or French toast, and sausage. I always thought the chow at our Battery was very good because we had excellent cooks.

After chow each morning we always checked the bulletin board to see what the orders of the day were. We had to read this to know what uniform to wear or what equipment we needed when reporting for the day's activities. At the end of the day's training we came back to the barracks, cleaned up and got ready for roll call again. After evening roll call we went to chow. Sometimes our evening roll call called for full dress inspection. All of this was in the name of discipline.

It was at one of these evening roll call sessions shortly after arriving at Fort Jackson that I received my first and only Summary Court Martial. During roll call, you must stand at attention with your eyes straight ahead without moving a muscle. I was standing in such a position when I saw something out of the corner of my eye. I quickly glanced in that direction. I no more than did this when I heard, "Private Roberts...report to quarters immediately after roll call." I wondered what was wrong and what I did. When I reported to the First Sergeant's office I had to see Captain Smith. The Captain told me that I was observed moving my eyes at roll call. He said it was within his authority to hold a Summary Court Martial and assess punishment. I, along with two other guys who were also being court martialed, was given one night of hard labor. Fortunately a summary court martial does not appear on a soldier's record.

After evening chow we changed into our fatigues and reported to the designated place for our punishment and were told to go to the supply room to requisition a shovel. Then we were told to start digging a hole. After the hole was over our heads, we were then told to fill it back up again. The Sergeant in charge of us just sneered at us throughout our ordeal. Carrying a rifle, he acted as though we were common prisoners. I never made that mistake again. What an embarrassing experience.

Our workweek began on Monday and ended on Saturday at noon with Sunday off. Occasionally we went on field problems over the weekend. Next to the Mess Hall was our Day Room, a small building where some of our training classes were held. During the off hours you could go to the day room to study your assignments, play cards, or write letters. I usually wrote my letters sitting on my bunk.

I wrote mushy letters almost everyday to Annie. Every other day I wrote to Mom and Dad. Mom wrote to me about the same number of times, but Dad hardly ever wrote to me. Occasionally he would add a few lines to Mom's letters. Mail was delivered to the barracks twice each day and was distributed by our battery clerk. When he came to the barracks area he hollered, "mail call" and all the guys went tumbling outside. The guys surrounded him like flies to honey, hoping to hear their names called and to receive a letter. Some of the letters had lipstick markings on the back of the envelope. Some soldiers rarely received any mail at all and never bothered to answer "mail call."

During the six weeks of basic training we were quarantined to the base. Now, we were ready for more advanced and specialized training.

Chapter 9

Advanced Field Training

Our training intensified. I kept my assignment as Scout Corporal with the Detail Section. Our section consisted of six enlisted men, including me, and the Reconnaissance Officer (1st Lieutenant) and the Forward Observer (2nd Lieutenant). Our job as the Detail Section was to survey the howitzers onto a target. One of the first things we were taught was how to apply logarithm tables and how to use the slide rule.

Each of us in our section was issued the *FM 6-40 Field Artillery Field Manual - Firing.* The manual contained 345 pages and covered everything about field artillery firing. We were told to read it, learn it, and memorize the main points for everyday use. This was to become our Bible, and we carried it on our person everywhere we went. It got wet, dog-eared, and worn from constant use. Our section equipment consisted of field glasses, aiming circle, range finder, a compass, and survey equipment (steel tapes and chains). We also had a topographical set, a large, wooden water-proof box that contained the slide rules, drawing boards, plotting equipment, pencils, pens, and maps.

By using survey equipment we were able to mathematically supply data to the Artillery Forward Observer (FO) or the Reconnaissance Officer (RO) and the Executive Officer (XO) at the gun position to effectively fire on a target.

The Instrument (or Detail) Section personnel were also responsible for going forward to the frontlines with the Infantry to observe the enemy. A target was either selected at random or at the request of the Infantry Officer or Divisional Fire Control Center, and this information was then telephoned or radioed to the gun battery XO for firing. A direct hit on the first round was rare. Additional commands are then sent back to the XO to adjust fire on the target. In combat, the target determines the type of shell, fuse, and powder charge, whether it was for an enemy tank, building, or personnel.

The field exercises lasted anywhere from over-night to several days. We always trained under battle conditions with simulated firing. As our field training progressed on the artillery range, live ammunition was used more and more. On the live ammunition exercises I was able to give the commands for firing and gained experience as a Forward Observer. I was able to see the results of my calculations and to determine how quickly I could adjust the shells on the target.

We began to train in our specific job assignments. My Military Occupational Skill (MOS) as a Scout Corporal, in addition to being part of the survey team, was to accompany an officer to find a new emplacement (position) for the Battery when it had to advance or retreat. Once we had found a new location that was suitable for setting the guns into position with proper protection and camouflage, it was my responsibility to return to the gun emplacement and lead the XO and the Firing Battery to the new location.

It sounds rather simple but during field problems (training), I had to apply my training and remember every detail of the path to the new position. Not getting lost proved rather difficult. I was not allowed to write anything down or draw pictures because it would reveal the position of the guns if I got captured. I learned to make mental checkpoints along the way by identifying a certain kind of tree, rock, gully, bridge, or bend in the road. Everything became a reference point when I was en route.

My Jeep driver and I led the way to the new gun position, followed by the XO in the vehicle directly behind us. This was quite a responsibility for an eighteen-year-old kid who had never been more than a hundred miles away from home. The first time we embarked into the field I was petrified. During my entire training I only lost the battery once while I was going to the new position.

During night field problems, our battery observed total blackout conditions. The only lights permitted were the vehicle "cat-eye" lights that provided a low watt slit-light, located just under each headlight, which could only be seen head-on for a very short distance.

The only time I lost the battery was on a night problem. There was no moon and it was pitch black. After locating the new position, I was able to find my way back to the battery without much difficulty, but on my way back to the new position I missed my checkpoint at the turnoff point. South Carolina is full of pine and scrub oak trees which have a tendency of looking alike at night. When I realized I missed my turnoff point, I then led the entire battery to an area where I thought I could turn them around, however, the trucks had a tough time turning, which delayed our firepower considerably. I really caught hell from my Battery Commander and I never got lost after that incident.

A few weeks into our training, each enlisted man was issued his side arm, the M1 caliber .30 carbine. Officers were issued the M1911A1 caliber .45 automatic pistol. All personnel were required to practice firing live ammunition at the target range and to "qualify" with their own weapon. Later, I was issued a Marksman medal to wear on my uniform and I was very proud to wear it.

We were also trained on the usage of other weapons, such as the 2.36-inch bazooka, an anti-tank rocket launcher, the M2 heavy barrel, caliber .50 machine gun, and the M-1 rifle.

Shortly after I completed my basic training, I received a disturbing letter from home. On May 10, 1943, my cousin George Burger, a P-38 fighter pilot, was reported "Missing in Action" by the War Department. George always had a passion for flying, even when we were kids. He learned how to fly at a very young age at the Hamilton airport in Hamilton, Ohio. In fact, he parachuted from an airplane when he was sixteen years old. George always liked thrills. He enlisted in the Air Force on January 10, 1942, right after Pearl Harbor, and received his "wings" on August 27th. He was first assigned to a bomber wing, but wanted to become a fighter pilot. He was sent to England on January 7, 1943. From there he was sent to an air base in Africa.

The only information that my Aunt and Uncle received from the War Department was that he was missing over the Mediterranean Sea on a mission as a fighter pilot. Later, the family was contacted by one of George's buddies who flew on the same mission. They were told that groups of P-38s were flying in formation when suddenly George peeled off from the group and was never heard from again. The wing commander tried to reach him by radio but received no answer. Since the group was flying on a mission, they could not follow George's plane. It was assumed that George crashed into the ocean and was killed or, if he did bail out, he died at sea. For many years the Burgers thought that he was on some kind of a secret mission and that he would show up one day. That never happened. George was the only one of my relations who died fighting for his country.

Our training continued to prepare us for combat that included gas mask training. Most nations agreed after World War I never to use gas in warfare again, but who can trust the enemy? I remembered stories at home about men in World War I who were gassed while fighting the Germans in France so I was prepared to listen.

Formal classroom training consisted of identifying all the different kinds of gasses and how they could be used, their effect on the human body, and the antidotes to administer in case of an attack. We were taught to identify the odor of gasses so if we smelled a certain odor creeping into our area we could identify the type and yell, "Gas!"

In small groups everyone had to take turns entering the gas chamber, but without our masks. This portion of the training exposed us to tear gas in order to familiarize us with the real effects of being gassed. Once the doors were opened we came tumbling out coughing and gasping for fresh air. Then we practiced going into the gas chamber, but with our gas mask in the carrying pouch. Once the gas was released and someone hollered "Gas!" we put our masks on as quickly as possible. This was a test to see if we knew how to put it on without any leakage around the face.

We were also exposed to mustard gas. Mustard gas was used during World War I by both the Allied and Axis forces. It was most commonly contained in artillery shells. Once the shells exploded, droplets of heavy yellowish liquid would land on the human skin and eat right into the flesh. If the fumes got into your lungs it would burn the inner lining. To experience the effect of mustard gas, a single 1/10-solution droplet was placed on the inner side of our forearm. We were told not to wash it off or to scratch it so we could feel the solution starting to work on our skin. The following day everyone had a large, ugly, yellow blister that lasted for many days.

On June 1, 1943, I was promoted to Private First Class (PFC). Again, I was proud of my recognition and promotion. I received a $4 per month raise in pay to $54. I was issued PFC stripes and I sewed them on all of my uniforms—each soldier was provided with his own sewing kit. I also continued serving as an "Acting Corporal."

One of my duties as barracks corporal was to make sure the lights were turned out at 9 p.m. I would blink the lights five minutes in advance, which represented the signal to get everything put away for the night. After five minutes had expired, I hollered "Lights Out!" and turned them off. No amount of pleading could make me keep them on. That was part of the disciplinary learning process.

On June 19, 1943 our first mass Division review (parade) was held on the *Ancrum Ferry Field* parade grounds at Ft. Jackson. The entire 106th Division participated in full dress. Soldiers wore their dress uniforms. The parade included the entire might of the Division such as trucks, howitzers, mortars, cannons, rifles, and machine guns, all of which were painted, polished, and shining. The Division band played and we marched to the cadence in perfect step. I was privileged to be the guidon carrier for our battery. It was quite an impressive ceremony and very inspiring.

I had never seen such "might" in all of my life and here I was a part of it. I was truly proud of being a soldier. I could feel my spine tingling as we marched past the reviewing stand where the "brass" stood and saluted as we marched past them. The parade was open to the public, press, relatives and friends of the Divisional personnel that day. Seeing the large display of men and material made me think about what the future held in store for us. *Where will our Division end up? Will it go overseas as a unit? Will it be a replacement Division? How much more training will we receive?* And I thought about death. These guys were still relatively young and they had loved ones at home, and each had a future in this world, just like me. I knew that some of us would not make it back home, but who will be the victims?

Death was brought home to our battery vividly one night while we were on one of our field problems. It was pitch black that night. As the Scout Corporal I had just returned to get the battery after reconnoitering a new forward gun position. As I led the battery to the new area, the lead truck turned off the road without incident. As the second truck pulled off the road, the driver turned his wheels too far, which caused the truck to slide sideways into a ditch. In doing so, the entire truck turned upside down causing the equipment and soldiers in the bed of the truck to spill on the ground. I had never heard such screaming before in all of my life. Any soldier in the immediate area rushed to the truck and helped physically lift the 4-ton Diamond "T" truck off the men trapped underneath. Unfortunately one of the men was riding on top and between the two spare truck wheels anchored to the back of the cab. He was wedged between the two wheels and was crushed to his death by the truck's steel cab top. When we pulled him out he was a mass of blood and there was no doubt in my mind that he was killed instantly. The field ambulance was called and he was pronounced dead upon arrival at the base hospital.

Even under such tragic circumstances, we were not allowed to turn the vehicle lights on so we could not see what we were doing. We had to work in almost complete darkness, except Captain Smith did permit us to use flashlights. That is when I saw how bloody the soldier was. We were on a simulated battle problem and we had to maintain strict security. You don't stop a war because somebody gets killed. Others were trapped under the bed of the truck. None of them were hurt seriously because the wood slats on the side of the truck kept most of the weight off them. The injured returned to our unit within the next few days after being evacuated.

That was my first experience in witnessing death in the Army. Unfortunately it would not be the last. I must admit that after the incident was all over I felt a little queasy. Our whole battery was shaken up and there were a couple of guys who actually had to be sent back to camp because they could not mentally deal with death. When trucks are in convoy it is standard operating procedure to have someone ride in that position on top of the truck spare wheels to serve as the "look out" for enemy aircraft. However, at night and under pitch-black darkness it is not required or even feasible. Why he was sitting in that position, no one will ever know.

There were a number of ways a soldier could get hurt while training. When we first began our obstacle course training we did it with an empty backpack, but as our training progressed more equipment was added until we finally traversed the course in full gear. The course required continuous running and surmounting various obstacles such as high walls, climbing ropes, swinging over water, crawling through large pipes, jumping over ditches, climbing ladders, crawling under barbed wire, and crawling over fences. This was one of the most grueling training exercises.

Another tough training exercise was the infiltration course. This exercise consisted of crawling under barbed wire on your belly and elbows with a full pack on your back, carrying your carbine while caliber .30 machine guns fired live ammunition just several inches over your head. The distance we had to crawl under these circumstances was about twenty yards. We had to crawl toward the machine gunner as he was firing. You had to keep your head and your butt down! The training was designed to give soldiers a feeling for the combat environment. The exercise mission was to get close enough to the machine gun emplacement and destroy it with a hand grenade.

Our battery did well in this exercise and no one got hurt. Unfortunately, throughout other divisions there were incidents where soldiers panicked and were accidentally shot when they stood up. Several were wounded and some were even killed.

We were also trained in hand-to-hand combat fighting. We were trained how to use our carbine as a defense weapon if we were ever to meet the enemy face-to-face. We learned how and where to strike in order to subdue or kill him, such as kicking him in the groin, how to strangle him with his own helmet, the pressure points in the human body to cause unconsciousness, and where to stab in order to kill. We practiced all of these moves on each other, just short of hurting the other guy. All of this training, we were told, was to develop the stamina and skill of each soldier so that he would out-march, outwit and out-fight the enemy.

On July 7, 1943, I was promoted to Corporal and I traded my PFC stripes for Corporal stripes. I had now become a Non-Commissioned Officer (Non-Com). Up to this point, not too many of the new recruits were upgraded to a Non-Com position. Most of the Non-Coms who trained us came from the 80th Infantry Division cadre. My pay was increased from $54 to $66 per month. This was almost equivalent to what I was making in civilian life and now I didn't have any expenses. Furthermore, I was given a private room on the second floor of our barracks and I continued to be in complete charge of our barracks floor.

All was not work and no play. After our six weeks of quarantine was over during basic training we were permitted passes to go into town. I usually went to town on Saturday nights with my buddies Carl Himberg, Bill Sewert and Ernie Tippet. On Sundays I remained in camp.

We picked up our passes at the First Sergeant's office, and then walked to a central location on the camp where Army trucks ran constant shuttles to take soldiers into the towns nearby. Most went to Columbia, South Carolina, which was not only the largest town but also the capitol of the state.

We always looked forward to walking the streets of downtown Columbia where the sidewalks were packed with service people including WACs (Women's Auxiliary Corps). Also with so many officers walking the streets saluting was a constant chore. Some officers were so "chicken" that if a soldier failed to salute them they took the soldier's name and reported him to his commanding officer for failing to salute an officer. I never missed once!

The three of us had a favorite restaurant we went to where we could get a huge steak dinner for $1. After dinner we walked the streets looking at the girls who were looking at the soldiers. Then we caught one of the last trucks back to camp.

Soon after being promoted to Corporal, I was notified that the Battery Commander wanted to see me. Every time I got the word that Captain Smith wanted to see me, I always asked myself, "What did I do wrong this time?" Guys were usually called before the Battery Commander when they had screwed up!

When I arrived, First Sergeant Lewis immediately sent me in to see Captain Smith. After I saluted and as I stood at attention, the Captain got up from behind his desk and closed the door that led into the First Sergeant's office. My Section Head, Staff Sergeant "Smokey" Stover, was also present. I was informed that I was being watched carefully and a thorough background check had been conducted on me. I was chosen to become a member of the CIC (Counter Intelligence Corps). My duties in the Battery Detail Section would remain unchanged, except that I was to conduct undercover work. I was not to tell anyone about my assignment, not the other officers, my fellow soldiers, the First Sergeant, and not even my family! I was forbidden to consult my Section Head unless it was urgent and only in strict confidence away from the battery site. I was duly sworn in by my Battery Commander to uphold the Constitution of the United States of America along with other verbiage.

My mission was to keep my eyes and ears open at all times around the barracks, in the field, in town, or wherever I may be, and report any revolutionary plans or espionage linked to either military or civilian personnel. I was to make myself available and join groups that were close-knit, to see what they were talking about and look for anything suspicious. If, in my judgment, any situation required investigation, I was to give names, dates, number of people, conditions, equipment, plot, plans, and any other detailed information I could provide. I was told that I could not refuse the assignment. I was selected based on my honesty, trustworthiness, as a good soldier, and a good American. This was very flattering and made me feel very good. I was also told that very few men could meet the rigid standards they placed on CIC members.

I was assigned a number that identified me as an agent and told to remember it but never to write it down. Every week I had to make a report and I disguised my number to a fictitiously named person. In letter format I submitted a coded message that indicated whether or not I had something to report. If I had something to report, I wrote, "Let's get together soon." A CIC agent would subsequently contact me in private. I was required to make a report even if I had nothing to report. I was provided with plain white paper with stamped envelopes, and each week I addressed an envelope to a different fictitious name, but assigned to the same P.O. Box number in Columbia, South Carolina. My assigned number was 1397 and I always included this number somewhere in my correspondence so they would know which agent had written the report. A typical sample letter I would write in making my report, if I had nothing to report, would look something like this:

July 19, 1943

Dear Joe,

How have you been? I have been fine. We sure are kept busy here at camp. Things have been very quiet, just the normal training and going into town on the weekends.

When I was in town over the weekend I did a little shopping. I tried to find a present for my girl friend's birthday. I looked at jewelry and what I liked was a bracelet. It cost $13.97, but that was more than I could afford. Instead I just settled on a scarf that costs much less.

Hope your family has been well too.

I just thought I would drop you a note and tell you that things are fine with me. As you know I am one who never writes long letters. I guess a short note is better than nothing at all.

So I will close, wishing you the best.

Your friend,
Pete

The key to the letter was the word "nothing," which meant that I had nothing to report and the $13.97 was my agent code number. My signature was always different, which corresponded to the fictitious person on the return address portion of the envelope.

I did exactly as I was instructed and revealed myself to no one. I mixed-in throughout the barracks, walked up to groups as they were talking on camp and in town, listened, and made mental notes of what I heard. I never uncovered anything that I felt was serious enough to report. I just heard the usual bitching from the GI's, but not to the point it required counter-espionage agents. Just before I left Ft. Jackson I had to report to Captain Smith with Sgt. Stover, my Section Head, where I was told that my CIC assignment had been terminated. I was commended for my faithfulness and how I performed my assignment. I was also told how much CIC headquarters appreciated my work. It was an honor for me to be selected for the assignment and I felt that I was making a profound contribution to my country.

In August 1943, the Army was looking for Field Artillery officer candidates to attend OCS (Officers Candidate School) at Ft. Sill, Oklahoma. Fortunately, my I.Q. test scores were high enough to make me eligible for consideration. I was contacted by my Reconnaissance Officer and asked if I had ever considered becoming an officer. He told me that I possessed the intelligence and leadership qualities that were essential in becoming an officer. While the idea had crossed my mind, I had to admit that

I never gave it any serious thought. He handed me an application and asked me to think it over. Being an officer had its privileges, but it also has its drawbacks. I liked what I was doing and the guys I was with. I also knew that upon graduation as a 2nd Lieutenant I would be vulnerable to immediate duty overseas as a Forward Observer (FO). We had heard that the average life expectancy of an FO in combat was ten minutes. I figured that my chances of surviving combat were better as an enlisted man, even though I was required to pull front-line observation duty. I tore up the application.

In August the Division authorized furloughs up to a maximum of ten days. Eligible soldiers were required to submit a written request. I made application and was authorized ten days, from September 1-10, which expired at midnight.

On September 1, 1943 I picked up my furlough papers from the First Sergeant and caught a camp bus headed for Columbia, South Carolina. I then walked to the train station to take the next train to Cincinnati, Ohio.

I was looking forward to seeing my parents and my girlfriend. Annie and I had been corresponding regularly and our "love letters" were a great morale builder for a soldier away from home. It sure was good to have a girl "back home." I had written my parents and my girlfriend telling them I was coming home and the dates of my furlough but I did not have an idea when I would arrive there.

The train took me to Union Terminal in Cincinnati, Ohio. I only walked a short distance to State Route 127, which was a main route through downtown Hamilton, Ohio. I began to hitchhike a ride and fortunately got a ride into Hamilton where I caught a city bus to my parents' home.

Right around the same time of my furlough, my brother Bob was in Dearborn, Michigan, attending the Naval Machinist Mate training school. After his graduation he would be assigned aboard a naval vessel, so when Mom told him that I was coming home on furlough, Bob made arrangements to get a three-day pass and come home. I had no idea of the arrangements and was pleasantly surprised when he also arrived home.

Our family had not been together for seven months, and Mom and Dad were especially proud of their uniformed sons. Bob's visit was rather short, but enjoyable. I spent a good portion of my furlough with Annie and we had a wonderful time together. We even spoke about a possible future life together. Annie's folks treated me like a long lost son.

I enjoyed my furlough very much, and in some ways I did not want to return to camp. But I missed the guys at camp and my new "Army life." After the tearful goodbyes, at the end of my furlough the bumpy train-ride arrived in Columbia, South Carolina late in the evening and I caught an Army bus back to camp.

Soon after returning from my furlough, the training intensified. I suspected that something was about to happen. After all, we had been in training for six months! Most of our original complement of officers and men had already been transferred out as replacements and were being sent overseas. We received new guys from other Army services who were not trained for combat, which hurt our efficiency. We had lost so many of our guys as replacements because the Army was suffering such heavy losses overseas.

About one month following my return from my furlough, I received my usual letter from Annie. When I opened the letter I was not greeted with the standard greeting, "My Dearest Darling Sweetheart." Instead it began with, "Dear Jack." Immediately I knew something was wrong. She explained that her former boyfriend had come home and they rekindled their love for one another. Needless to say, I was crushed. Like a lot of other guys in the service, I had received the infamous "Dear John" letter. But life goes on and I buried myself in my Army career.

Around December 1st we got the word that our Division would be going on maneuvers. Maneuvers are designed to test the endurance of a unit under field conditions that closely resemble actual combat conditions. The only difference is that no live ammunition is used. Maneuvers lasted for several weeks and pitted the "Reds" against the "Blues."

One day in December, I was summoned to the Battery Commander's office. Captain Smith informed me that I had been hand picked to join the "Umpire's Staff" for the maneuvers. He explained that my selection was because I displayed a thorough understanding of field artillery and a talent for analyzing situations. The Umpire Staff was a handpicked group of officers and enlisted men whose role was important in making the maneuvers a success. Since live ammunition was not used, the Umpires' decisions and actions would be critical in determining which side would "win the war." If Captain Smith was trying to make me feel good, he did.

The Umpire's school was one of the most grueling schools I ever attended while in the Service. We were repeatedly tested on our technical artillery knowledge and our ability to make decisions. We were taught that we could never make mistakes. Even if we made a bad call, we could not deviate from our decision. After two weeks time my schooling had been completed and I resumed training with my unit.

In preparation for the maneuvers, most of the training was now conducted in a classroom. Lt. Divencenzo conducted one of the final classroom training sessions that addressed to "Kill or Be Killed." Seated outside our barracks, he told a group of us to remember all the training that we had received. He added that one day in the near future we would need the training to survive in combat. He proceeded to tell us what the enemy would do to us, and why we had to win the war. Then he got into the gory detail of how to kill and maim another human.

The Lieutenant got so emotionally worked up that during his presentation he started to choke up and then he began to cry. He simply walked off and left us sitting there. Lt. Divencenzo was a devout Catholic. I am convinced that by looking over our youthful and innocent faces, and telling us how to kill someone, must have really got to him. After he departed we just looked at each other. When the message began to sink in, we just got up and walked back to the barracks. His lecture could not have been more impressive.

For Christmas, my first away from home, we were given Christmas Day off so we could go to our denominational religious services on base. I went to Mass with a couple of the other Catholic soldiers in our barracks. Frankly, I think we would have been better served if we had been kept busy. Many of the guys, including me, began to think about home. The next day, however, it was back to normal.

On Christmas Day a notice was posted on the bulletin board that General Dwight D. Eisenhower was named Supreme Commander of all the European armed forces. We knew that it would not be much longer before an invasion would take place aimed at the heart of Germany to defeat Adolf Hitler.

Each Battery had a day room, which had recreational items such as boxing gloves, baseball equipment, horseshoes, etc. On New Year's Eve, a group of guys were crowded around two guys in the room that wore boxing gloves and were sparring with one another. One boxer was Pvt. Good who recently transferred into our Battery. Good was a professional fighter from New York and held a junior title. He was taking on all comers.

A couple of the guys goaded me into putting on the gloves with Good. I said I had never boxed before, but they said it was only in good fun. Good promised not to hurt me, and since the gloves were large and well padded, I thought what the heck. Good and I sparred around for a few minutes and then he started to get a little rough. I became irritated and I must have clipped him a little harder than I should have, when all at once he hauled off and belted me. I was hit with such force that I flew across the room and into the arms of a couple of guys that kept me from falling to the floor.

The fact that Good hit me so hard made some of the other guys mad. I was well liked and got along with the guys. As I regained my sense of balance, a big Tennessee "hillbilly" by the name of Nipper said to me, "Gimmee them damn things."

Nipper always seemed to like me. He was about twenty-six years old and about six and one-half feet tall. After Nipper put on the gloves all of the guys gathered to cheer him on. Everyone wanted Nipper to get the best of Good but we all knew that Good was a professionally trained fighter, and Nipper was not. Good had finesse whereas Nipper had none. He was a farm boy and developed his fighting skills during bar room brawls in Tennessee. What a match this turned out to be.

Nipper and Good fought for a short time. Good was laughing, jabbing, poking, and dancing all around Nipper. Nipper moved very slow and deliberately, never smiling or saying a word. He kept both eyes on Good. Then, all of a sudden, Nipper's right glove came up from the floor with a "haymaker" (upper cut) that caught Good on the jaw and sent him flying clear across the floor. Good was out cold. The guys really cheered for Nipper. Too bad Good could not hear the jubilation. Nipper looked at me, smiled, and said,

"I guess that'll teach the S.O.B!"

After a while Good finally came around. From then on he was not as cocky, and I never put the gloves on again either. What a way to end 1943.

Chapter 10

Maneuvers In Tennessee

On January 2, 1944 the Division was scheduled to leave Ft. Jackson, South Carolina for maneuvers somewhere near Nashville, Tennessee. Maneuvers were to last approximately two months and were to be divided into eight field exercises lasting one week each. My section head, S/Sgt. Stover, advised me that I would be assigned to Battery "C" until we reached our destination in Tennessee where I would then join the Umpire Staff, based at Camp Forest, Tennessee. The news of the pending maneuvers was greeted with mixed emotions. We knew we would go into combat as a Division, however, we had no idea whether it would be in the Pacific or the European Theater of operations.

After two bivouacs we arrived at our destination outside of Murfreesboro, Tennessee. The following morning I bade farewell to my buddies and was driven to Camp Forest for my assignment to the Umpire Pool. Frankly, I questioned whether I would ever return to the 106th. Upon arrival, an Umpire Staff member greeted me. I was shown to my assigned barracks, told where the chow hall was located, and where to report after lunch for a group meeting that day. My immediate superior officer was 1st Lt. Babcock. I felt lucky for the assignment, considering the rest of the Division would live in the field for the entire two months while we were on maneuvers. At least I was afforded the comfort of the barracks over the weekend.

Members of the Umpire Staff were assigned white armbands for identification. In addition, I was assigned a Jeep driver and a radio operator. My equipment consisted of a Jeep with a ten-foot radio antenna and a white flag attached to the top of it, which identified it as an Umpire vehicle and made it immune from being destroyed during the simulated combat.

Mass meetings were held with the Umpire crews to ensure a clear understanding of the simulated war between the Red and Blue forces. We were taught strategy, methods of troop movement, deliverance of firepower and mechanization and aerial attacks.

I was the umpire in charge of my crew. We received topographic maps of the "battlefield" terrain with various marked coordinates, allowing us to follow the simulated fighting. In addition, I received a compass, field glasses, a flashlight, a box of "cherry bombs," matches, a pencil, notebook, a clip board, and paper. We were also issued a supply of tags that were printed with the words "dead" or "wounded." In addition to my assignment as an artillery umpire, other appropriate umpire crews were assigned to specific branches of the Army, such as the infantry, armory, engineers, etc. The umpire's job was to make decisions in the field, using special formulas for calculations, in order to determine the extent of damage to equipment, loss of lives, or the number of soldiers wounded or killed.

Each of the eight field exercises had a different objective for each week, although they were all somewhat similar in nature. During the first week of exercise, the 106th was assigned to the Blue Force XII Corps, and included the 78th Infantry Division, one tank Battalion and two Tank Destroyer Battalions, and supported by the Blue tactical air division. The Corps' mission was to advance north along an east-west line through Murfreesboro, attack the opposing Red Force defensive line, and be prepared for advancement on Hartsville, Tennessee. The Red Force consisted of the 26th Infantry Division with similar supporting forces including the Red Tactical Air Division.

My job was to cover an area bounded by coordinates shown on the battle map. We listened to our radio continuously for artillery fire that would fall in our area, and we never left the radio during the entire week. I had to determine if the Blue or Red forces were firing their artillery, and register the information if it affected my area, such as the number of shells or volleys being fired, the type of shell burst and the exact coordinates where the shells were falling. Then I directed the driver to that location. When I arrived at the coordinates where the simulated shells were landing, I mathematically calculated the amount of fire that fell in the area and determined the scope of the damage. Simultaneously, the driver jumped out of the Jeep and ignited a cherry bomb to advise the troops in the area that artillery was falling. Immediately I calculated the number of soldiers that were either killed or wounded, percentage wise, in the area and advised the officer or NCO in charge as to the damages and casualties. The "dead" or "wounded" tags were then placed on the men chosen by the Officer in Charge (OIC) and myself. As we began to place tags on the casualties it was amusing to see the number of soldiers who volunteered to be killed or wounded. I could readily understand this due to the terrible weather. We slept where we could and ate "C" and "K" rations the entire week

"C" rations came in a pack containing two cans. Each can was about the size of a small can of soup. One can contained a staple food, such as pork and beans or beef stew and hash. These items were better if heated, but most were eaten cold because we had no heating facility. However, those who were fortunate enough to have access to an Army vehicle could heat the food on its engine block. The second can in the pack contained such items as hard biscuits, cigarettes, a fruit bar, and toilet paper. A small can opener was also included in the packet.

"K" rations came in a box about the size of a "Cracker Jack" box. The box was covered in a heavy brown wax to keep all thc moisture out. Inside were a variety of edibles, depending on the box you obtained, such as a small can of scrambled eggs and bacon, a chocolate "D" bar or a fruit bar. Although none of the food could be found in a first class restaurant, if you were starving for nourishment, the food actually tasted good.

The "dead" soldiers who had to be returned to base camp were not allowed to be used again for action during the balance of that week's field exercise. The wounded were sent to the rear echelon medical center and, depending on the extent of their wounds, some of the soldiers were able to return to the fighting. Following my decisions and while I was recording the information in my notebook, the radio operator contacted the Umpire Headquarters and rcported everything that had taken place. This information was then released to both the Red and Blue forces. This method allowed each side to know how much equipment and how many casualties had been suffered on both sides and the progress they were making against each other.

We attended our weekly weekend mass meeting in one of the auditoriums at Camp Forest to listen to the top brass of the Umpire Staff talk to us about the past week's exercise and about our assignment in the next problem. These meetings were also orientation sessions where we learned about the events in both theaters of war overseas. At one of the sessions in early March we learned that 800 B-17 Flying Fortresses had attacked Berlin, Germany on March 6, 1944, and dropped over 2,000 tons of bombs on the city. The cheers that came from the crowd of soldiers were deafening.

I was usually free after Umpire meetings on Saturday at Camp Forest. On occasions I would go to Indianapolis on a Saturday night by myself for dinner and then to the United Service Organization (USO) for recreation. On Sunday, I went to Mass at the camp's chapel and then spent the rest of the day getting the crew, supplies and the Jeep ready for our next assignment and driving to the map coordinates that were scheduled as my next assignment.

On one Saturday on our way to Camp Forest following our field problem and before an Umpire meeting I decided to stop in for a haircut in Lebanon, Tennessee. The town was rather small with one main street down the center of town. It was crowded with local townspeople and we drove down the street looking for a barbershop. Military rules were clear that you never smoked while in a military vehicle and especially in our vehicle because we had a number of cherry bombs, which were highly explosive and could be disastrous if a fire started, lying on the backseat floor.

Right in the middle of town one of the cherry bombs ignited right under my seat. Its ball of fire could not get out of the Jeep so it flailed around the floor of the Jeep igniting the other cherry bombs. The driver slammed on the brakes and the three of us jumped out of the Jeep, which was by then surrounded by a cloud of smoke as a fire had broke out inside the vehicle. Someone called the local fire department but as soon as I jumped out I grabbed the fire extinguisher, which was mounted on the Jeep and proceeded to extinguish the fire. By the time the firemen arrived I had the fire pretty much under control. I was worried that the gas tank would explode and injure everyone, especially the crowd that had started to curiously gather around to see what all the noise and fuss was about.

I apologized to the fire department and by that time the Military Police were on the scene. I had to make a complete report as to what happened. The only thing I could figure out was that somehow ignition took place accidentally. The MPs wanted to know if anyone was smoking in the vehicle. Neither my driver nor I were smoking and when we turned to the radio operator he admitted to lighting a cigarette and then when he thought I was about to catch him smoking he dropped the cigarette on the floor and ignited a fuse on one of the cherry bombs.

There was no haircut for me that day. The Jeep was capable of being driven and we took it to the motor pool at camp and turned it in. I reported the incident when I turned the Jeep into the motor pool. A big blowup took place and I was threatened with being court martialed for destroying a military vehicle because the Jeep was under my command. I had to report to my superior officer about what happened and he was furious. I was told that I would have to pay for the Jeep's damage. Obviously I was very upset.

I never lost my job as an Umpire and was issued a different Jeep to continue my work. Weeks went by and I never heard anything about a court martial nor making restitution for the damaged Jeep.

Every aspect of the maneuvers was realistic. Even though the fighting was simulated, one usually got the idea that this was pretty close to the real thing. There were forced marches and river crossings. There was mire, mud, muck, slime, rain, sleet, snow, fog, and every form of inhospitable weather you could imagine.

The Air Force fighter planes "strafed" troop and equipment concentrations. There were even real "gas" (tear gas) attacks in various areas where the affected soldiers had to use their gas masks. Everyone was aware that no matter how difficult the exercises were, the actions taken on a basic level could mean life or death in actual combat.

On February 1st the Divisional strength was 912 officers and 12,556 enlisted men. Within the next few weeks the 106th Division transferred 871 well-trained enlisted men out of the divisional ranks. However, 1,214 new men came in, of which 1,157 came from Army Specialized Training Program schools. They were very intelligent men but they lacked combat training. These were the men who would eventually go overseas and into combat without adequate training. The personnel changes were just one of the first steps that reduced the fighting efficiency of the Division. These decisions, along with others yet to come, may have cost the Division more human lives when it went into battle.

Strangely enough, the seventh exercise from March 13-17 started off in a snowstorm that changed to rain and sleet, with frost forming on the soft mud, and ending in thunder and lightning. This was a real dress rehearsal for the battles to come in the Ardennes forest in Belgium. In retrospect, one could say that nature was doing its best to acclimate our Division.

The eighth and final exercise was also fought in probably the worst weather conditions of the entire maneuvers.

When the final exercise was over our umpire group returned to Camp Forest. We turned in our gear and equipment and got ready to return to our units. I was concerned that I might be reassigned and would not be able to return to the 106th Division. At the final mass meeting, the entire group of umpires were commended for a job well done and told we would all return to our own units. Despite destroying a Jeep, Lt. Babcock, my superior officer, was very appreciative for the job we did for him.

In retrospect, I would say the two months I spent on maneuvers in Tennessee were the worst two months I had spent in the Army. Both mentally and physically because of the extended periods in the field, the gruesome weather, the wet clothes, the lack of sleep, food rations, and the job under stressful conditions. The pressure definitely took its toll on me as I lost quite a bit of weight and caught several colds in the field. Doing my job and not feeling well under such circumstances was rough. In spite of it all, I enjoyed the assignment and the authority, plus I learned a lot. Most of all, I survived.

As we gathered to return to our own units, I thanked my driver and radio operator for a job well done. I then climbed aboard the back of a GMC truck with several other guys, along with our duffel bags, and we were returned to our units. I sure was glad to be heading back to Battery "C" and to see my friends. I had no contact with anyone from my unit for the two months I was gone. I was delighted to see Bill Sewert, Carl Himberg, Ernie Tippett, and some of the other guys and they seemed glad to see me too. They all kidded me about being on a soft job for two months. In some ways I did have it better, but in some ways a whole lot worse.

As soon as I unloaded my gear I reported to my Battery Commander, Captain Smith. He wanted to hear about some of my experiences, how I liked it, and what I had learned. He thanked me for taking the assignment and assured me that my selection was based on my understanding for artillery, and he knew it would be an educational experience for me. As a nineteen-year-old kid, the assignment was a great responsibility. My decisions had a direct impact on the "wins" and "losses" in the simulated war. I learned more as an umpire than I could ever have learned as a Scout Corporal with my battery on maneuvers. Captain Smith did me a great favor by placing me on this assignment. My later survival in the Ardennes must be credited to this experience.

Captain Smith also told me that our Division was going to Camp Atterbury, Indiana, located just south of Indianapolis. He and I were mutually delighted about our next camp assignment since he was from Greenwood, Indiana, which is located just a few miles south of Indianapolis, and I was only about a hundred miles from my home in Hamilton, Ohio. Now I knew that I could get home periodically over the weekends and see Mom and Dad before we went overseas.

Chapter 11

A Wartime Romance

Spring was in the air when we loaded onto our vehicles and headed for Camp Atterbury, Indiana. On March 27, 1944 we left the Tennessee area for what would be our final training within the United States before going overseas.

Camp Atterbury was located about 30 miles south of Indianapolis, Indiana. Named after General W. W. Atterbury, former Director of the Army Expeditionary Forces (AEF) in World War I, it was one of the newest and largest training camps in the country—it covered over 40,000 acres. After World War II it became a training camp for National Guard units from several mid-west states. Our arrival at Camp Atterbury meant that we were getting ready to go overseas. We didn't know if our destination would be in Europe or the Pacific. Worst of all we had no idea of when we were going to depart.

Our training at Camp Atterbury was intensive because of the massive exit of Divisional officers and enlisted personnel who were being sent overseas. As a result, the new replacements received accelerated field training throughout the summer months. Just when we thought the Division had established a solid training foundation shortly after having completed maneuvers, the additional shift of personnel took place.

The day we arrived at Camp Atterbury we unloaded our equipment and we were assigned to our barracks. One of the first things I did was call Mom and Dad to tell them that I had arrived at Camp Atterbury. They were delighted that I was so close to home.

When the bulletin board had a notice stating that our Division was authorizing furloughs, I immediately applied and requested that it begin as soon as possible. I wanted a pass right away because so many of our guys were being transferred out to replacement depots, so I figured that if I did not go on furlough soon, I just might not get the chance at all. To my delight, I saw my name published for authorization for a ten-day furlough, from Thursday, April 6th, to Saturday, April 15th.

Bill Sewert and I each obtained a furlough. He lived in Lewisburg, Ohio and I lived in Hamilton, Ohio about forty miles south of Bill. We took the camp bus into Indianapolis and began to hitchhike. Wearing a uniform in those days made it easy to get a ride. We were lucky soon after raising our thumbs because the first guy who stopped was going to Dayton, Ohio. After we were dropped off, I began thumbing for a ride and it took a couple of local jaunts to get to Hamilton where I took a city bus to my parents' home.

My parents were glad to see me. This was the first time I had been home in seven months. My furlough was an adventure. I visited family, friends and former coworkers but there was not much to do. All of my buddies were in the service like I was. However, one day I decided to go into town and used my brother Bob's 1939 Buick sedan. Since this was the only transportation my parents had I knew I had to be careful. It had just stopped raining and as I turned a corner the car went into a skid. The front bumper of the Buick scraped the entire left side of a Studebaker that was parked along the curb. The skid resulted from a lack of tread on the Buick's tires. The Studebaker belonged to the owner of a bar behind where the car was parked. I found the owner and explained what had happened and he was not very happy. I told him the insurance would pay for damages and my father took care of everything when I returned to camp.

The day our furloughs expired I made arrangements to meet Bill Sewert at a Greyhound Bus station near his home to ride back to Indianapolis together. There we caught a military bus back to camp and just arrived at our barracks a few minutes before our midnight deadline, or else we would have been Absent Without Leave (AWOL).

The following week after returning to camp from my furlough I received a letter during "mail call" from a girl I once worked with at Keiser Clothing Co. Her name was Mary Lou Staarmann. Mary Lou had quit her job while I still worked there for a better job as a stenographer with a local insurance company in Hamilton. The letter was friendly and mostly small talk but mentioned that she heard that I had been home on furlough and stationed nearby. She said that if I ever got home on another furlough or a weekend pass I should give her a call. I wrote back and told her I would do just that.

The following week our field exercise was a special event and we had to do our best. We went into the field with our full combat gear where we were visited and observed by Under Secretary of War, Robert P. Patterson. He called it a "great performance." This made everyone feel pretty good, especially since we had many new soldiers in the division who were still being trained for combat.

By the time we met the needs of the replacement depots, the 106th Infantry Division transferred out 7,247, or 60% of its enlisted strength. This removal of more than one-half of the division's trained strength, and replacing it with unfamiliar men, will not produce good results. Expecting the division to be prepared for battle, as a combat team just cannot be done no matter how good the replacements or the cadre are because the cohesion that is developed during rigorous training for effective teamwork, esprit de corps, and pride in the organization are missing. This transfer out of men was the direct opposite of the purpose our division was formed originally in March 1943. Of the seven soldiers who were in my original Detail Section, only Carl Himberg and myself had founding status. The War Department's method of stripping our division had a demoralizing effect on all of us, and it remained with the division. To think of who would be fighting by your side against a well-trained enemy made one concerned.

Early on the morning of June 6, 1944, an invasion fleet of some 4,000 ships stormed the Normandy beaches of France and delivered thousands of American and British Divisions, followed by artillery, tanks, vehicles and other war supplies and equipment. During the first week, the Allies drove about twenty miles inland. Casualties for the landing were heavy—40,000 out of some 600,000 men. The war was now about to change drastically. I had a gut feeling that it would not be very long before the 106th Infantry Division would be in the thick of battle in Europe.

For the next couple of weeks we were extremely busy at camp. During the week it seemed as though we were always in the field on some kind of training exercise because of the influx of the unseasoned personnel.

Over the weekend of June 15th we prepared for a Divisional review at the Camp Atterbury parade grounds. The review included everyone in the Division, with all our combat gear and equipment. This meant that the vehicles, half-tracks, howitzers, and cannons had to be either cleaned or painted and in tip-top condition. We spent a lot of time preparing for the review. The press, radio, local, state and federal government officials, Army brass, and even the 106th Infantry Division soldier's family members were invited to the parade. What a spectacular event it was.

It was not until the latter part of June that I had the opportunity to go home again. I called Mary Lou Staarmann after I arrived home and asked if she was busy. She wasn't, so I offered to take her out for a Coke. She obliged and I picked her up in Bob's car. I had not seen Mary Lou since my buddy Eppy's going away party put on by the workers at the Keiser Clothing store and I must admit that I was nervous and excited, even though there was nothing romantic between us. We went to a bar that had a small band playing and we just sat in a booth, talking and listening to the music. When I took Mary Lou home, I took her to the door and lightly kissed her goodnight.

We then began our wartime correspondence. We began writing to each other steadily. After my next visit home Mary Lou gave me a couple of pictures of herself, one for my wallet and one in a small leather frame for me to place on top of my wall locker in the barracks. From then on, I tried to get home as often as I could.

On the bulletin board at camp I noticed we were scheduled for a survivor training exercise that consisted of jumping from a tower into a lake. On base there was a small lake and a tower that was built over the water itself. The tower had a steep ramp that ran from the ground level to the top of the tower. Every soldier, dressed in full gear with backpack and carbine, was required to climb to the top and then jump approximately twenty feet into the water and swim to shore. I did not know how to swim and I was petrified of the water. The exercise was to simulate abandoning a ship going overseas if the enemy torpedoed the ship.

The day before the tower exercise I was summoned to the First Sergeant's office and told that I was being placed on special assignment duty the very next day! The special assignment was to assist in indoor training exercises for the artillery officers. This meant I would not be required to jump off the water tower. What a relief that was.

The special training assignment encompassed a simulated artillery firing range inside a building. A high platform on one side allowed the officers to stand and overlook a large 3-D miniature landscape, which contained houses, trucks, tanks, personnel, and roads. The trees, grass, hills, houses, tanks, personnel, vehicles, were all painted and built to scale. It was a marvelous piece of craftsmanship and looked very authentic. The landscape was anywhere from one foot to several feet over our heads, depending on the terrain of the landscape, and it was marked with coordinates, identical to an artillery terrain map. The base of the entire landscape was made of heavy netting.

Our job was to work beneath the mesh landscape and to receive the commands from the artillery officer who was simulating firing howitzer shells at a particular target above our heads. We mathematically transposed his commands to the proper coordinates where the round was intended to land. Using a gadget that sent out a puff of white smoke through the mesh landscape, we simulated an impact "burst." The officer, observing the smoke, knew exactly where the round had landed. If the officer missed the target, he telephoned additional commands to us for adjustment. The new commands were followed until he accomplished his mission. I enjoyed the special assignment, especially since it kept me from jumping off the high tower into the water.

After having my first date with Mary Lou and having started a very earnest correspondence with her, I traveled home every possible weekend. My method of travel rotated between going by train, bus and hitchhiking. I could feel a "wartime romance" developing between us that was growing from infatuation to a love relationship in a very short period of time.

In checking the bulletin board one morning a notice stated that a limited number of furloughs were to be granted over the next few weeks. Bill Sewert and I put in for one just as soon as the notice went up. Again we were fortunate enough to be among the first wave of soldiers to be granted a furlough. This time going home we took the train, Bill to Dayton, Ohio and me to Cincinnati, Ohio.

While on furlough I spent most of my time with Mary Lou. I did visit other people but I was now in love with Mary Lou and that made a big difference. Becoming involved with her I felt confident that she would not be writing me a "Dear John" letter. I was a little reluctant at first to get involved with her having been dumped by Annie a few months before that when I was at Fort Jackson, South Carolina.

During that summer, the June 6th Invasion at Normandy and a few other developments around the world gave the impression that the war in Europe was making progress. On July 25, 1944, the German defenses around Normandy crumbled after constant attack by the Allied forces. On August 14th, the U.S. Government lifted production restrictions on vacuum cleaners, electric ranges and cooking utensils, unless they would be needed for the war effort. Just two weeks later, Allied Forces entered and liberated Paris from German occupational forces.

After returning to Camp Atterbury from our furlough we heard a rumor from fairly reliable sources that our Division was destined for frontline duty in Europe. This word brought the war closer to us on a personal basis.

On August 10th, I turned nineteen-years of age and went home on a weekend pass. After our world-wind romance, I made up my mind that I wanted to marry Mary Lou Staarmann. Now all I needed to do was ask her. I arrived home on Saturday just in time for dinner, after which I was drying the dishes for Mom.

It was then that I asked her, "What would you say if I told you that I wanted to give Mary Lou an engagement ring and ask her to marry me?"

My Mother froze and stared into the dishpan. She then raised her head and looked me right in the eye and with a concerned voice she asked, "Don't you think you are bit young for such a big responsibility at a time like this?"

I had expected to hear something along those lines, but I told my Mother that I did not intend on getting married before I went overseas, and that I would wait until I returned home from the war. She said that Mary Lou was a very nice girl, and since she came from such a good family, she would welcome her into ours if that was what I wanted. Both Mom and Dad liked Mary Lou very much.

My Father's reaction was almost the same. His only wish was that I wait until I returned from the war before getting hitched. To my surprise, my mother offered to give me one of her diamond rings that she had inherited from her mother, my Grandmother Mary Wolke.

The following weekend I was unable to get a weekend pass but I did manage to get a one-day pass for Sunday. After Sunday mass, I decided to go into town with a buddy and we walked the streets until we stopped at a sign that read, "Record your own voice - $1.00." An automatic voice-recording machine provided three minutes to record anything you wanted to say. When I finished, a small six-inch record dropped into a box, which I mailed home to Mom and Dad. After I went overseas, Mom, Dad and Mary Lou played it every so often, just to hear my voice. I guess it turned out to be a good investment.

About the second week in September a notice was posted on the bulletin board stating that no more furloughs or weekend passes would be issued, except for emergencies. However, we could still get passes into town for an evening. We knew that this meant that we were getting closer to our departure from Camp Atterbury. I called Mom and told her that with all likelihood I would not be home again until the war was over. This meant that I could not give the ring to Mary Lou unless Mom and Dad would bring Mary Lou to Camp Atterbury, for the last time, where I could propose to her.

A few days later the Division was placed on full alert. This meant that everything had to be ready for departure overseas. While we were kept in the dark about our port of debarkation, we heard that New York and Boston were the only ports large enough to handle a full Division of troops and its equipment. Only our government issued essentials could be taken with us and anything else had to be either shipped home or thrown away. Any pictures or letters that we took along had to have the names and addresses obliterated so we would not be identified as a resident of a certain area in the United States. New dog tags were issued that only listed our name, Army serial number, religion, and blood type. While your old dog tags had to be turned in, like most of the guys, I told the Supply Sergeant I had lost mine and he didn't care. I sent my old tags home.

On September 19, 1944, the big day had finally arrived. Mom, Dad, and Mary Lou were coming to Camp Atterbury. I did not sleep very much after talking with Mom and wondering if I was doing the right thing at such a young age of nineteen years. *Would Mary Lou accept my proposal? Would I return home from the war? Would she marry me out of pity if I were maimed and required constant care? And if she accepts my proposal, is it fair to ask her not to date anyone else for the period of time while I am gone? That could be months or even years!*

I quickly put these negative thoughts out of my mind and looked at the brighter side of life; live it one day at a time! After the 9 a.m. mass on Sunday, I proceeded to the visitor center where I was going to meet Mom, Dad, and Mary Lou. As I look back on the situation, I never once discussed my proposed intentions with Mary Lou's parents, which was the proper thing to do in those days.

They arrived at the visitor center shortly before noon and I took them to lunch at the Post Exchange (PX). When Mary Lou wasn't looking, Mom slipped me the box that contained the engagement ring and I slipped it inside my shirt.

After we had eaten, I excused Mary Lou and myself. Dad had parked the car in back of the PX, and this offered me a little privacy. Mary Lou asked what I wanted to show her. As she got in the car, I closed the door and walked around to the other side. I got in, and without saying another word, I handed her the ring box. I tried to propose but my mouth opened and nothing came out because my mouth was as dry as cotton. I swallowed a couple of times, between Mary Lou's gulps of surprise, I then finally said, "Will you marry me?"

I had never seen anyone as surprised as Mary Lou in my life. She was flabbergasted and sat with her mouth wide open and nothing came out. She hesitated for a few seconds and tears came to her eyes. She answered, "Yes!" and we kissed, hugged, and cried. After a few minutes we had calmed down and we talked very seriously about what the ring and the engagement meant. She said she would accept, but only on the condition that we would wait to marry until after I had returned from overseas. I agreed with her and told her that I had promised Mom and Dad the same. Behind PX No. 19, at about 1 p.m. on Sunday, September 19, 1944, Cpl. Jack Roberts and Mary Lou Staarmann became engaged at Camp Atterbury, Indiana.

When we returned to my folks we were both smiling from ear to ear. Mom and Dad smiled and in my choked up words I said, "She said yes!" Mom and Dad congratulated us and they were happy to welcome her as a future member of our family.

Soon, reality began to set in. There I was only nineteen years old and engaged to be married with a girl from home, just before I was going overseas. I was duty bound and convinced the war had to be won for the future of our country, our very own existence, and that of our families and I had to do my part to make it all happen. I considered my current home to be with the Army and I had to make the best of it. I felt very patriotic.

Three weeks after becoming engaged I left Camp Atterbury for the East Coast and headed to Europe. During the weeks leading up to our departure we prepared for the move. We were confined to the camp and spent most of our time making our equipment combat ready according to the table of equipment (T/E). I called my parents and Mary Lou just before leaving camp. The final conversation was difficult and very emotional.

Chapter 12

Camp Myles Standish

On October 6-7, 1944 we secured our equipment on our assigned vehicles and prepared them for shipment. The next day, trucks supplied by the base Quartermaster's Corps arrived at our battery where we loaded for the ride to the camp railhead. When we got there, it was obvious that the railroad companies had leased their worst cars to the military for troop transport.

The train loaded with soldiers chugged out of Camp Atterbury and on its way to the East Coast. As might be expected, whenever we stopped near a town, some of the guys tried to find an open bar and get a beer or a shot of whiskey. The Military Police (MPs) had their hands full in trying to prevent the soldiers from running off. Because they were unable to stop all of them, they had to round up the guys before the train pulled out.

We continued to speculate as to where our destination would be. It had to be either Boston, New York City, or to some other major port. We followed the pattern of the train station signs and we knew for sure that we were headed for the East Coast.

We were responsible for making our own preparations for the nights rest, but the noise of the railroad tracks made sleeping impossible. Carl Himberg and I bunked together on the top bunk of a sleeper car but we were awake most of the night talking about our families and hometowns, speculating about our involvement in the war, and peeking out the window to look for clues as to our location.

On the second day our train passed through towns in New York, Connecticut, Rhode Island, and finally Massachusetts. On October 10th, we stopped somewhere outside of Boston. We were ordered to pack our belongings and be ready to move out for Camp Myles Standish. We now knew our exact destination.

Camp Myles Standish was an old embarkation and debarkation camp for soldiers during World War I. During World War II it was mainly used as a springboard for troops waiting to go overseas. Experienced personnel who knew how to handle large numbers of transient troops ran the camp. It contained PX buildings, chapels, barbershops, mess halls and theaters. When we arrived we had no idea how long we would be staying before we sailed for foreign soil. As it turned out, we would be here for thirty-one days.

We were assigned to barracks that had either double- or triple-decker bunk beds. I got the lower bunk of a double, and Bill Sewert was my bunkmate. Many of the guys were assigned to work details, such as Kitchen Police (KP) or guard duty. Here I was assigned KP duty. This was the very first and last time I ever did KP.

While we did not have any equipment to maintain, we spent our time attending orientation classes that were held in the mess halls or camp theaters. The Army brass told us about the war and what to expect in combat. We saw maps of the frontlines in Europe and heard about survival, "kill or be killed!" We had our daily roll calls and we did our daily calisthenics to stay in shape physically and mentally.

Liberty passes were issued to go into Boston, New York, Providence, or one of the other cities nearby. I was told that the wharf area in the city of Providence was beautiful and had a nice restaurant right along the water. It was only about fifty miles from Boston by bus and you could easily make it in one day. The following Sunday I got a pass and went to Providence by myself. Although I should have, I never told anyone where I was going because I wanted to be by myself for a change.

The soldier who suggested that I visit the Providence wharf certainly knew what he was talking about. I was dumbfounded with the beauty of it all; the beautiful weather, ships, sailboats, and sea gulls. Having never seen the water before, let alone sailboats and other watercraft, this sight left me breathless. I felt as though the whole world belonged to me because I didn't see many military personnel. I had dinner at a restaurant on the wharf and thought about my family, my past years, and my engagement to Mary Lou. I simply enjoyed my new experience. I was so impressed with my solitary excursion that I did the same thing on the following Sunday. I wanted to go again on the third week, but no more passes were issued and I was confined to the camp area. This meant that the time to "ship out" was near at hand.

I wrote to my fiancée every day, and periodically to my folks, and told them of my experiences. When we left Camp Atterbury we were given our overseas Army Post Office address (APO #443 c/o Postmaster, New York, NY), which I sent home to the folks and Mary Lou. Over the next several months some of our mail was lost. I could tell that some of Mary Lou's and Mom's letters were missing by what they wrote. Apparently some of my letters to them were lost as well. I tried to keep Mom, Dad, and Mary Lou informed but after arriving overseas our mail was subject to censorship.

At one of our final orientation sessions at Camp Miles Standish we were told that our next destination would be England. Our mission was to relieve a Division and to occupy a frontline position in Germany! We were not told which Infantry Division we would relieve or where in Germany we would occupy at the front. A select group of soldiers from the 106th Division had already sailed for Europe as the "Advance Party." Their mission was to make any necessary arrangements for the remainder of the Division when they arrived in England.

During a battery orientation session we received word from our Battery Commander, Capt. Robert Smith, that all of the Divisional Artillery would sail from Gloucester, Massachusetts, aboard the USCGSS WAKEFIELD. On November 9th, we prepared our belongings to board ship. The 106th Infantry Division sailed in increments whereby on November 10, 1944, the Divisional Artillery sailed for Europe. Special troops within the Division, such as Ordnance, Medical, and the Quartermasters would join us on our ship. The 2nd Battalion, 424th Infantry Regiment, left New York on October 18th on board the QUEEN MARY. The remaining regimental battalions and the entire 422nd Infantry Regiment left on October 20th on board the USS AQUITANIA.

Chapter 13

Sailing On The High Seas

On Friday morning, November 10, 1944, we were finally summoned for a final roll call outside the barracks to ensure that no soldier was Absent Without Leave (AWOL). None of the guys were joking or cutting up as we usually experienced. Indeed, the day was somber for all of us and the fact that it was raining did not help.

We marched to a special troop train as the rain continued to fall. The train ride was a few miles from Camp Myles Standish to our port of embarkation at Gloucester, Massachusetts. When I got off the train I saw the largest ship I had ever set eyes on. This ship would take us across the Atlantic Ocean to Europe. The ship was named the USCGSS WAKEFIELD, and was actually the former luxury liner MANHATTAN that had been converted into a troop transport ship for soldiers crossing the Atlantic. It was one of the largest ships ever built in America. The ship was moored right next to the pier and tied up with ropes several inches thick. A long gangplank extended from the ship to the pier. The ship towered several stories into the air, and the hull, deck and rigging were painted gray. After boarding we found out that the gray color was a camouflage to blend in with the ocean and to make it less likely to be seen by enemy planes, ships, or submarines.

I had mixed feelings about going to Europe. I was happy about the opportunity to visit foreign countries, but since I had to go into action first, that made it all somewhat disconcerting. As a twenty-year-old who was looking forward to adventure, I was eager to sail across the ocean on a big ship. But if there was a way that I could have stayed on the ship and returned back to the States immediately thereafter, I could have enjoyed the trip even more!

The quarters on troop ships were designed to transport as many soldiers as possible at one time, thus forfeiting any comfort. When I crawled into my bunk there was no more than

15 inches between my head and the bunk above it. The bunks were made just large enough for a medium sized person. The addition of our duffle bag made for a very tight fit.

Hanging from our bunk was a life jacket. While at sea, the life preserver was to be worn at all times. It was to be kept at our sides when sleeping or washing.

At about 4:30 p.m. we could feel the ship beginning to move. A lot of the soldiers and I were on deck to observe our departure. I wanted to get the feeling and the sight of the ocean. I heard the noise of the engines as the bow of the ship pushed the seawater aside with the aid of the tugboats. By the time we got out and into the ocean it was already dark. I was truly amazed when I looked over the rail of the ship and saw the sparkling phosphorus in the water. It looked as though millions of tiny little lights were being churned up from under the sea. It was beautiful.

Our ship was scheduled to sail late in the afternoon so that when it entered the sea it could sail a great distance under the cover of darkness. After all, German submarines preyed on U.S. ships off the coast. More disconcerting was the news that our ship would cross the Atlantic unescorted. In the past, Naval gunboats had escorted most of the troop ships, however now the escort ships were engaged in other parts of the world. Moreover, since the U.S. Navy had destroyed so many German warships and submarines, it was now felt that our ship could "risk" the trip without a naval escort. It is interesting to note that because the USCGSS WAKEFIELD was not under escort, it sailed on a zigzag course. By applying such a radical zigzag course, the maneuver made it difficult for a German submarine to track the ship and fire a torpedo.

I did not know exactly how many troops were on the USCGSS WAKEFIELD, but there had to be several thousand. I toured the main deck and it appeared that there were not enough lifeboats to hold everyone in case we really did have to abandon ship.

The first night I slept fairly well. I woke up periodically when the ship pitched and rolled through the water as the seas became rougher.

I spent as much time as possible during the entire trip topside. I enjoyed the experience of being up on deck, and besides, the air was fresher than below deck. I was fascinated with the ocean and the ship's movement. I looked for whales or any kind of large fish, and was thrilled when I saw porpoises and "flying" fish. On occasions, the porpoises swam along side our ship for a considerable time before they veered off and disappeared.

At sea, I wrote to Mary Lou and the folks several times. Service personnel now used the one page overseas "V" mail stationery, which was 8-1/2 X 10 inches. Once we arrived in England the letter was photographed and reduced to 4 X 5 inches before mailing. I knew that my letters would not be mailed until we arrived in Europe but I wanted to give Mary Lou and the folks an account of my adventure at sea. Since our letters were now subject to censorship we were told to be careful as to what we wrote. If the censor read something that seemed to be "classified" the censor would physically cut out the word or sentence.

The Atlantic Ocean is vulnerable to violent storms during the month of November. During our voyage at sea we saw and felt some of the worst storms that anyone could experience. As the ship pitched and rolled, soldiers in the hull of the ship were actually thrown from one side to another. We hung on for dear life or chanced being thrown out of the bunk and on to the deck (floor). While sleeping I wedged my duffel bag and life preserver on the open side and lay next to the bulkhead (wall) to prevent myself from falling out of my bunk. Since my bunk was the second from the top I would have a distance to fall.

As I stood topside during a storm and watched the ocean swells, the wind and rain blew into my face so hard that I could barely see the bow of the ship. The ship's Captain maneuvered the ship directly into the swells to avoid capsizing. Some of the swells I observed were twenty to thirty feet high. As I watched this before me, a wall of water soared high over the bow of the ship. I thought for sure that I would be washed over the side when it crashed onto the deck, but I held onto the rigging for dear life. Other swells were so large and powerful that they could lift the ship right out of the water. After the ship passed over the swell it plunged down into a trough. Riding out a storm like that was just like being on a huge roller coaster ride. I loved every minute of the excitement!

Most everything I did and saw I wrote home about. At the very least, my experiences were not boring. I roamed the entire deck and all of the ship's compartments throughout the voyage to Europe. I believe I visited every place on the ship except the engine room.

One learns how to exist on a troop ship very quickly. Only two meals were served daily—a big breakfast and an early dinner—because of the massive number of soldiers on board the ship. We ate in the galley in shifts and you ate whatever they slopped on your tray. The tray was made of metal with depressed sections.

The tray was carried to any table where there was an opening to place your tray. The high tables were also constructed of metal and anchored to the deck. The motion of the ship made it difficult to stand and eat. During a violent storm with the ship's rocking motion it was almost impossible. You had to balance your body, hold on to the table and your tray to keep it from sliding off onto the floor, which happened frequently, and still try to eat. Mealtime was a challenge.

What made it worse was when soldiers got seasick. Sometimes they threw up on their food in their tray of food or on the metal table and sometimes on the deck. Walking on the deck where men threw-up or spilled their food made it quite slippery, which was another challenge to survive in the galley. You sure had to watch your step. The stench of the fowl air from the toilets, human bodies, and vomit and food odors was terrible. One had to have a strong stomach to choke down a meal. I never got seasick and I did eat my meals on time but it was not very pleasant. Meal times were indeed a challenge.

Showers were out in the open as were the toilets. The water used for showering was salt water pumped from the ocean and unheated. Shaving was also difficult using a razor with cold salt water and a dull scratched metal mirror anchored to the bulkhead.

Another challenge was going to the toilet, which was one big room, which also housed the showers and washbasins. The toilets were anchored to the bulkhead and the seats consisted of a long wooden plank with several holes cut in the wood. Under the plank (seats) was a long metal trough with water to catch the waste matter. One soon learns that you never sit on either end of the row of open holes because when the ship rocked the water rushed from one end of the trough to the other and when it hit either end the water and waste splashed up and drenched your bare bottom.

On the afternoon of November 16th, a destroyer escort met the USCGSS WAKEFIELD and guided her into St. George's Channel. Naval escorts provided all troop ships that were arriving or departing with protection against any German submarine that might be in the annex. In addition they help the troop ships navigate safely through the minefields that were laid off the coast. After entering the channel our ship anchored for the night.

The next morning we could see the coast of Wales from the deck. We still did not know where we would dock in England. A British pilot boat came along side our ship and several men came aboard. In the afternoon we could hear and feel the engines winding up as we ambled through the channel toward our docking destination. This was my first sight of Britain and it would become my first experience to set foot on foreign soil.

As the USCGSS WAKEFIELD sailed ever so slowly up the channel, we observed the British anti-aircraft batteries that were located along the shoreline. The channel was a vital British shipping supply line that the Germans tried to destroy several times during the war. As we approached our docking station, everyone was ordered below and to return to their compartments. Our gear was gathered and made ready to disembark. One of the British men, who boarded our ship from the pilot boat, came through our compartment. We stopped him and asked him where we were going to dock. He answered, "Liverpool." He spoke with a typical British accent that we all found amusing. I had only heard such an accent before in the movies.

We had to wait for quite a long time before it was our turn to disembark from the ship. My unit Battery "C" was one of the last to leave. Overall, it was a wonderful experience crossing the Atlantic Ocean on a troop ship, in spite of the bad weather, inconvenience, lousy food, odors, discomfort, and poor facilities. It was an experience that I will never forget.

Chapter 14

Combat Readiness In Britain

It was about 4 p.m. by the time the USCGSS WAKEFIELD maneuvered into its harbor berth in the port of Liverpool. At about 11 p.m., November 16, 1944, I stepped foot on foreign soil for the very first time. The night was smog-filled, misty, and cold. A penetrating chill went clear through my body and into my bones. But at least we were back on land again.

All of Britain, especially the harbor area, was under constant black out conditions because it was vulnerable and under constant threat of air raids. England had already suffered massive German bombing attacks as well as the V-1 and V-2 rocket attacks.

The Divisional Units took a train to their new destinations. The entire 106th Infantry Division was to be billeted in British camps near the towns of Gloucester, Adderbury, Banbury, and Chipping Norton, about 300 kilometers (180 miles) from Liverpool. London was about 80 kilometers (48 miles) from our new locale. The 592nd Field Artillery Battalion was assigned to barracks in Adderbury. Gloucester was the nearest town of any size.

We arrived at Adderbury in the early morning hours and were shown to our quarters where the bunks were decked two high. The barracks were old and built of brick and stone with walls several inches thick. They had high ceilings, large rooms, large toilet stalls with high partitions, and long windows with glass that was painted black to keep the light from showing.

Our training consisted of calisthenics and we learned more about the Germans, such as equipment and uniform recognition, and what to expect from their fighting tactics.

After several days we received word that liberty passes were available that allowed us to make excursions into the nearby towns. One evening Bill Sewert, Carl Himberg and I requested a pass to the town of Gloucester. Before leaving for town we converted our U.S. dollars into British pounds. Trucks were made available to take the soldiers into town.

Downtown Gloucester was dark, except for a few dim lights along the streets. Whenever a door to a pub opened, it spilled a stream of light into the dark and brightened the fog-covered sidewalk. The streets were crowded with American and some British soldiers. Most of the soldiers congregated in the pubs once they arrived in town because this was the first opportunity since leaving the States to purchase any kind of alcohol. We settled on a particular pub and, after a short wait, found a table in the middle of the pub from where we could see everything and order a pint of ale.

We talked with some of the local residents in the bar. The ravages of war had certainly been felt all over Britain. As Americans, we were welcomed wherever we went.

My recollection of Britain during the two weeks I was there was not favorable. I only remember the darkness and the cold wet fog. I saw very little of the countryside and contact with the towns-people was limited to some of the patrons in the pubs. The only time that I saw sunshine since I left the United States was when I saw the sun set over the ocean as we neared the coast of England just before it began to rain once again.

I occupied the remainder of my time in Britain at night by reading and writing letters to Mary Lou, Mom and Dad, my brother Bob, and other relatives and friends. Shortly after arriving at the camp, all the mail that had been sent to us while we were on board ship for the past seven days was distributed. I received many letters that took me a considerable time to respond to.

I was overcome by an eerie feeling after about a week. Our equipment had been checked and loaded into vehicles, and we knew which vehicle we would ride in. We knew everything except the departure date and where we would board a ship to sail across the English Channel. The departure date had to be rapidly approaching. The old familiar thoughts began to return, such as *What might I encounter when we reach the frontlines in Germany? Where will we go into position on the frontlines? What is it really like up there? What will the weather and living conditions be like?* These were all questions, but there were no answers. The unknown is cruel and agonizing, and it can cause anguish in even the best of men. Questions of a personal nature came to my mind such as: Will I make it through the war? Will I be killed, maimed, captured or injured? When will the war be over? If I am captured, will I be treated well, starved, shot, or beaten to death? At our orientation sessions I remembered seeing U.S. Army films, in addition to some captured German films, which showed some very gruesome pictures how captured soldiers were treated. These thoughts, along with the miserable weather, did not help troop morale.

On November 30th, we received the official word that we had been anticipating. The 106th Infantry Division was to move out on December 1-2 for our respective ports of embarkation. The Divisional Artillery was scheduled to proceed to Weymouth, at the lower tip of Britain, and board ships to cross the English Channel to France. Our Detail Section was to ride in the back of a ¾-ton Dodge truck, commonly called a Weapons Carrier. The distance from Gloucester to Weymouth was about 150 kilometers (90 miles).

On December 2nd, we loaded up on our assigned vehicles and moved to the harbor where several Landing Ship Tanks (LST) were waiting. We received coffee and donuts, life preservers, and seasickness pills. We heard that the channel could be a rough ride on an LST.

Those who were lucky were assigned quarter that were much better than the facilities on the USCGSS WAKEFIELD. My buddies and I were among the less fortunate. Like most others, we ended up sleeping inside our vehicle in the hull of the ship. Some of the guys slept on the deck itself. After entering the channel a short distance, the LST dropped anchor and we sat there for the rest of the day. On the morning of December 3rd, the LST pulled up anchor and steamed across the English Channel. We dropped anchor that evening about 5 miles from the port of Le Harve in France. Le Harve was such a busy port that we had to wait our turn to enter. No one bargained for the bad weather that had blown in while we were anchored in the channel.

It was never intended for us to remain on the LST for any length of time so the galley ran out of food. Supplies of "K" and

“C” rations were brought on board to supplement the food shortages.

Chapter 15

France – An Ungodly Ride

Sometime during the night of our third day on the Channel, the winds let up somewhat and the rough seas died down enough to permit our LST to haul anchor the next morning. In the early morning hours of December 6, 1944, our LST entered the mouth of the Seine River at Le Harve, France and began its journey on the waterway eastward toward the city of Rouen, our destination.

The ride on the Seine was very smooth. Much different than the English Channel where we constantly bounced around. The English Channel is reputed to be one of the "uneasiest" bodies of water in the world.

We traveled about 42 miles (or 70 kilometers) on the river. At that particular time of year France was nothing more than barren farmlands covered with snow. The only city of any size that we passed along the way was Caudebec, which could be seen in the distance from the ship.

Around noon we arrived at Rouen, the city where Joan of Arc was burned at the stake. S/Sgt. Stover told us to "mount up" and wait for our turn to drive off the ship. He said we would travel in convoy from the ship to our first bivouac, somewhere in France. Shortly after getting into our vehicles, we could hear and feel the engines of the LST slow down and in a matter of minutes we could feel the ship bump and shudder as the bow of the ship struck the shore.

After the LST was secured, the mammoth steel doors in the hull opened wide and the ramps were lowered into place. One by one, each vehicle started its engine and took its turn driving from the ship. When our turn arrived to depart our weapons carrier eased out of the ship's opening and down the ramp. The crew directing the landing hollered to our driver to put the vehicle in four-wheel drive because other vehicles before us had created deep ruts in the muddy shore. We inched our way onto the slippery muddy soil of France, followed a shoreline path, and made our way to the main road.

When we drove onto the soil of France, we knew we had a long ride before reaching our next destination in Germany, which was 500 miles (800 kilometers) away. Wind, snow, and sleet penetrated the convoy on route to the bivouac area.

The close-knit groups in my section riding with me were Carl Himberg, George Peterson, Bill Sewert, and Leonard Weiner. Our driver was Terrill Rigdon and riding with him in the cab was our section head, Staff Sergeant "Smokey" Stover. Only about half of all the guys in Battery "C" were of the original group that took basic training together at Fort Jackson, South Carolina. The other half came to us as replacements at Camp Atterbury, following maneuvers. Although I liked the guys, many of them lacked sufficient artillery and combat training. This worried me.

We traveled the main roads in convoy and they seemed to be in fairly good shape, although I could see where the German Army, when advancing or retreating across France, had repaired some of the bridges and roads from the earlier scars of war. Throughout the day, we passed through many towns and villages. Since our weapons carrier was covered with a canvas top and siding, our only view was out the rear of the truck. We could see where we had been but not where we were going. Sometimes townspeople stood along the roadside and waved to us. Many French people loved the Americans, remembering their recent liberation from German occupation.

While in convoy, if a guy had to relieve himself between "piss calls," he stepped out the back of the truck with one foot on the tongue of the trailer near the hitch while the other foot remained inside on the bed of the truck. One of us would hold onto him while he used one hand to hold on to the rear "roof bow" so he wouldn't fall out on the road as the truck traveled along. His other hand had to guide the stream of urine. At one time or another throughout the trip across France, I was in such a position as were my buddies.

This relief procedure worked well. One time, however, our field telephone operator George Peterson experienced some difficulty. During his urination ritual, he straddled the tailgate and was hanging on the roof bow for dear life. He was in the process of relieving himself as we passed one of the military checkpoints where a high-ranking officer was stationed. To review his troops Lt. Colonel Richard Weber was standing up in his command car by the roadside watching our convoy pass. When Peterson saw the Colonel, he instantly remembered his early military training to salute all officers and let go of his dong to salute Colonel Weber while the stream flew through the air.

We heard Peterson say out loud, "Oh…shit!" We all looked out the back of the truck to see what happened. We began to laugh like hell, all except Peterson. Peterson worried that the Colonel might report the incident to Captain Smith, our Battery Commander. From the big grin on the Colonel's face we felt pretty sure he wouldn't, especially after the Colonel returned Peterson's salute. We never heard about the incident after that.

The first stop on our trek was Limesy, a bivouac area in France. We arrived there at 4 p.m. Mud, cold, and miserable weather served as our welcoming party. Upon entering the bivouac location, each vehicle had to be parked in its designated area. All vehicles were spaced apart in case of an enemy attack.

A couple of the battery vehicles got mired in the mud and needed to be wrenched free. One happened to be the kitchen truck and was freed rather quickly. The guys made sure of that, as we were all quite hungry for a hot meal.

We really had a good sergeant over our section. S/Sgt. "Smokey" Stover was a likeable and reasonable twenty-eight-year old. The guys in the Detail Section back at Fort Jackson pinned the nickname "Smokey" on Stover. The name Smokey came from an old cartoon character, which happened to be a bumbling firefighter called "Smokey Stover." Giving nicknames was quite prevalent in the Army. Some soldiers even had obscene nicknames that they seemed to enjoy.

Sgt. Stover was a regular Army soldier who was making the service his career. Sgt. Stover and I had a good rapport. He was my immediate superior contact when I was affiliated with the CIC at Fort Jackson, South Carolina.

When Sgt. Stover had to tell us to pitch our pup tent and sleep in our bedroll on the muddy ground, he did it in such a manner that we knew he would allow whatever other means of sleeping we might decide on that night. No one relished the idea of rolling out his bedroll in the mud.

One of the officers came around and told us that we must dig a "fox hole" before we "sacked in" for the night for our own protection. Everyone just ignored his order because none of the officers attempted to dig one. The only hole that we dug was the "slit" trench for the latrine and a "sump" for the garbage generated by the kitchen and leftover scraps generated from mess kits. A few soldiers were given this detail work.

After the kitchen truck was winched from the mud, we ate our first hot meal in five days. We had the same cooks from Fort Jackson. S/Sgt. John H. Jones and Sgt. Hertko were the main cooks with Cpl. Elwood Lorah and Pfc. Aaron Hamblin as second cooks. These guys were usually right on the ball. Whenever they had the opportunity they always prepared hot food for the guys.

In order to get our "hot" food, we had to stand in the chow line with our mess kit, canteen cup, knife, fork and spoon, and submerge our cold eating utensils in a vat of boiling hot water. By the time we finally reached the back of the kitchen truck where the chow was being served and then found a place to eat it, the food and our utensils were fairly cold.

The hot meal served that night did help the morale somewhat. I stood up and ate my meal as fast as I could while it was still halfway warm, while trying to shield my food from the rain by hunching my body over my mess kit. Even so, the cold water dripped off my helmet and into my food. This whole first night was just a sample of what was in store for us. After eating, I hurriedly washed and scalded my mess kit and went back to the weapons carrier. Each time we crawled over the tailgate and into the back of the truck. We tracked in mud with our combat boots. There were no provisions for us to wash since the bivouac area was merely a large wooded field where vehicles could pull off the road and we could sleep for the night.

We were told that we had to shave before we shoved off on the next leg of our trip the next morning. The kitchen furnished hot water. We dipped our canteen cup into the tub of hot water and poured it into our steel helmet shell to take back to the truck. I shaved using my safety razor and shaving cream from my "dopp" kit along with a metal mirror. We had the option of shaving in the morning but since I wasn't sure what would happen then, I decided to shave in the rain. Even though it was almost dark, I felt where the whiskers were. We all looked and felt "cruddy." The shave felt surprisingly refreshing.

Those of us who were assigned to our weapons carrier decided that we would sleep sitting up in the back of the truck. After all, we were getting used to sleeping in that position from the days spent on the LST. The canvas top and sides covering our vehicle gave us the protection from sleet and rain but not from the cold air.

I ended up sleeping in a corner of the truck where I could rest my body against a wooden bow that held up the canvas covering. Sgt. Stover and Rigdon, the driver, also crawled in the back of the truck to sleep. We were wedged shoulder to shoulder. Our body heat in the cramped quarters was an asset.

I must admit my morale sagged after that first night. I began to wonder about the kind of life I was about to live while in Europe, especially with the full blast of winter approaching. I knew there would be no barracks to sleep in or to keep warm, no showers, no laundry, no clean clothes, and to face an enemy who wanted to kill me.

It did not take very long before I dropped off to sleep. I catnapped most of the night. The sound of the sleet hitting the canvas top of the truck must have lulled me to sleep. I admit that I prayed a lot, at every chance I got. As we bounced along riding in the back of the truck throughout our trip, I said the rosary on my fingers many times. I talked to God and I sincerely felt He heard me. I was thoroughly convinced that He heard me after guiding me through combat.

Early the next morning I awoke to the sound of men stirring around the bivouac area. I crawled out from the back of the truck to stretch and go to the latrine. Straddling a slit trench with cold wind blowing on your butt is not very comfortable to say the least. The rain and sleet had stopped while the cold blistered on. It was just before daybreak and chow was about to be served, so I grabbed my mess kit and went to breakfast. I was glad that I shaved the night before because the morning air was much colder. Our convoy would be back on the road soon after daybreak for the next leg of our trek across France.

Shortly after chow we were issued ammunition for our carbines. Each of us was issued five clips. Each clip had twelve rounds of ammunition. We were told to keep four clips in our ammunition belt and the fifth was to be placed in the carbine with strict orders not to put a bullet into the firing chamber and to keep the safety lock on the carbine until we enter the combat zone. We were also told to keep the weapon on our person at all times. Never leave it no matter where we go or what we do. The issuance of live ammunition made me contemplate the reality of facing the enemy. I grappled with grueling thoughts as I loaded the weapon. *Will I be able to kill another human being? Under what circumstances?* My questions were again left unanswered.

We were ordered to mount up in our respective vehicles. Our battery had to wait its turn to pull out of the Limesy bivouac area since many units of the Division Artillery were in the same convoy. It must have been around mid-morning before we left for the next bivouac area at Rossee in Belgium.

In order to keep warm in the back of the truck I wore my overcoat, wool gloves, and wool-stocking hat under my helmet. We talked little on the truck. As I looked at the somber faces of my fellow soldiers, each guy was staring into space and appeared to be deep in thought. I guess I was not the only worried soul. None of us wanted to talk openly about fighting at the frontlines. Either we didn't know what to speculate about or we didn't want to because we were afraid. Periodically, one of the guys would crack a joke while the rest of us forced a laugh.

It was December 7th and my thoughts wandered to that same day in 1941. I was at Bill Webster's house, comfortably seated at the kitchen table playing cards with Bill when we heard the news that the Japanese bombed Pearl Harbor. As I walked home, I wondered how the news might affect my future. Little did I know that three years later I would be seated in a truck and headed for the German frontlines. Fate is an odd thing.

Our convoy arrived at Rossee, Belgium that night at around ten o'clock. The weather was much colder and snow covered the landscape. Underneath the snow, the terrain was just as muddy as Limesy. We went through the same routine: hot meal, shaved, and dug a latrine and sump. We slept sitting up in the back of the truck, shoulder to shoulder. My feet felt numb, so I ruffled through my duffle bag for some dry socks. It is amazing what rest and dry socks will do for a person's well being. Our convoy left late the next day to our final bivouac area near St. Vith, Belgium. We were deployed to relieve the 12th Field Artillery Battalion of the 2nd Infantry Division. The heavy snow and wind continued.

As we headed for Germany, the forests grew more dense. The wind blew off the blanket of snow that covered the evergreens. The trees looked black and I thought they looked eerie.

There is no soldier who participated in that cold comfortless trek across France will ever forget it. I thought about Mary Lou, Mom, Dad, and Bob. In my mind, I congratulated Bob for joining the Navy. At least he never had to experience this kind of miserable living.

My Division found itself astride the Siegfried Line that runs along the crest of the Schnee Eifel Mountains, a hogback ridge nosing southwesterly down from the Eifel area and pointing to the junction of the Belgium-Luxembourg-Germany boundaries.

In taking over for the 2nd Infantry Division, our division found itself spread out over a twenty-five-mile front, which is almost three times as much territory that should be assigned to one single Infantry Division. Our defense was very thin and our forces were overextended. The 2nd Division was anxious to get out now that some of their replacements entered the area.

The twenty-five mile front that the 106th Division took over projected into enemy lines some eight miles at its deepest point-from the town of Lanzerath on the north to Grosskampenberg on the south. My unit, "C" Battery went into position on the north edge of the village of Laudesville, which sat in a ravine, where several barns and farmhouses were located. Our detail, wire, and radio sections took over one of the farmhouses used for billeting by the 12th Field Artillery.

My section took over the second floor of the farmhouse. There were a few feather beds for us to sleep on. We finally got our duffel bags and bedrolls. There are no linens at the frontlines. On the first floor of the farmhouse was a small kitchen, without the furniture, but it did contain a wood-burning stove and we kept the fire going by burning logs from fallen trees. We all took our turn at guard duty and stoking the fire. The battery kitchen truck was located in the general vicinity of all four guns that were in firing position and meals were served at normal eating hours. We ate in shifts so there would never be too many soldiers congregated in one location at one time in case enemy artillery shells would land in our area.

We went into position on December 10, 1944 with Capt. Robert W. Smith as our Battery Commander, 1st Lt. Walter D. Sohier our Reconnaissance officer, and 1st Lt. Rex C. Matson our forward observer. 1st Lt. James R. Kennedy and 1st Lt. A.V. Siekierski, the Executive Officer manned at the guns.

The next several days were spent checking over our equipment to make sure that all continued in combat readiness. The poor visibility prevented the howitzers from being fired by the various artillery batteries. The forward observation post could not see where the shells would land. Members of the detail, wire, and radio sections were divided into forward observer teams that would take turns at the frontline post at Roth, Germany. Teams were relieved in the morning. I would go forward with my team on December 16th, six days later. Little did I realize when I received my assignment, what was in store for me.

Not all went well with the light artillery battalions when they went into position. The gunners and the cannoneers asked the executive officer where the main supply of Howitzer ammunition was. The problem started in England and was not settled until we reached the frontlines. Personnel of the Supply

Depot assured Divisional Artillery that they had plenty of ammo in Belgium.

Nevertheless despite efforts, not a single round could be found and all three light Field Artillery Battalions (105mm-589th, 590th and the 591st) trundled into their positions without it. In fact, Divisional Artillery Commander Brigadier General Leo T. McMahon, who was in charge of all artillery, had to decline to relieve one of the 2nd Division's light artillery battalions on December 9th because of these circumstances.

The 2nd Division's medium artillery (155mm) had plenty of ammunition. The ammunition "trains" (truck convoys) began to arrive from as far away as Liege, Belgium and by December 14th, all battalions had their basic load. The ammunition was mixed which added to the difficulty of accuracy when fired.

I had my first guard duty after our second night in Laudesfeld, Germany from 2 to 4 a.m. It gave me an eerie feeling. Being brand new at the front in a strange country, in a strange area, can have an effect on the human mind. We heard rumors about the enemy infiltrating into the American positions at the front and that land mines may have been planted as the enemy retreated months before. Such stories as well as rumors has a way of being magnified in the mind especially at 2 a.m. when it is absolutely quiet, except for the occasional burst of enemy or American gunfire or artillery fire in the distance.

The air was crispy cold that night and as I walked my patrol, the crunch of the snow underfoot seemed quite loud. I walked to keep from freezing. Periodically, I stopped to listen and with a constant keen eye I just kept looking for anything unusual moving in the area. Sometimes you think you hear and see things that are just not there. Your mind can play tricks on you and rational thinking doesn't always prevail.

My paranoia was given fodder having learned about "Bed Check Charlie." This is what the Allied forces called a German pilot that flew an airplane over the frontlines at night, just above low hanging clouds to harass the troops. He was known to drop "butterfly" bombs that were small explosives. I never saw Bed Check Charlie but I heard him and envisioned flocks of butterfly bombs, parachute wings flapping in the wind, headed for our position.

On our third day at the frontlines, we received mail. Since we had not received any mail since we left England, some two weeks before, all of the letters had piled up. What a great day and a real morale builder. After going into position at Laudesfeld, I wrote Mary Lou every day. We were told to destroy our incoming mail after we had read it, so it would not fall into enemy hands.

Our Forward Observer group, in position in an abandoned bunker at Roth, reported some small arms fire and German patrol activity. Our 423rd Infantry Regiment sent several patrols out as far as 800 yards without enemy contact, though sporadic fire was received. The 422nd experienced some evidence of enemy activity. The noise of motors welled in the trees. Each day we gathered with our section leader for an orientation session. We all needed to be currently updated on the extent of the situation. From the information we received, the sector was quiet.

There was some evidence of complacency mixed with insecurity among the men. This was our first contact with the enemy. Rumors magnified in our minds. Corps Intelligence had informed our headquarters that the Germans might be playing transcriptions over loudspeaker amplification systems to simulate a massing of forces. Our division with its newly arrived troops would lean heavily on the opinions of the higher command. Perhaps the rose-tinted glasses of the Corps Intelligence personnel had much influence on our Divisional Intelligence operations.

The 12th Field Artillery officially turned over the observation post at Roth to our battery on December 15th. I was scheduled to go forward with our party the next morning at 8 a.m on December 16th. As a Scout Corporal, it was my assignment to help observe and seek out enemy targets at the observation post.

Our vehicles and gun emplacements located in Laudesfeld, Germany were equipped with two-way radios, but we maintained radio silence for fear that the enemy could monitor our channels. We communicated by telephone between the forward observer post and the Executive Officer.

I did not have to stand guard duty the night of December 15th, so I had a good night's rest until 5:30 the next morning.

Chapter 16

The Battle of The Bulge

At 5:30 a.m. on December 16, 1944, deafening artillery explosions nearby suddenly awakened all of Battery "C." Those who were sleeping as well as those who were at their battle positions wanted to find out what was happening. After all, this area was supposed to be a quiet sector of the Ardennes.

Our Detail Section, quartered on the second floor of the farmhouse, scrambled out of our bedrolls and tumbled downstairs still half asleep and out in the open barnyard looking for our answers. We found our Section Head S/Sgt. Stover and began asking him a lot of questions, but he had not idea what was happening either. Our Battery, as well as the rest of the 106th Infantry Division, was under a massive artillery attack! The look on everyone's face ranged from fright and bewilderment to anger.

The attack on our battery position was only a small part of the larger German Counter-Offensive, code named *Wacht am Rhein*, designed to sever the Allied lines of communication by concentrating three armies along an eighty-five-mile front, cross over the Meuse River between Liege and Namur in Belgium, bypassing the capital city of Brussels, and recapturing the important logistical port of Antwerp, Belgium. Here in this picturesque winter countryside, blanketed by white snow and covered by a gray sky canopy, the German positions in the north had placed the 18th Volksgrenadier-Division (VGD) almost directly east of St. Vith and our Division was in its path.

The battle plan of the 18th VGD was to move along the Auw-Schoenberg-St. Vith road. Behind the 18th VGD, the *Fuhrer Begleit-Brigade* (FBB), a detachment of the elite Army Panzer grenadier-Division *Grob Deutschland*, would move west while holding the right flank of the 18th VGD. The German's path of attack would roll right over our battery (C/592).

The German attack was mighty. They fired numerous artillery calibers at the Americans, including the 106th Infantry Division, which came amidst red, green and white flares that flickered through the early morning darkness lighting the areas under the overcast skies. The sudden impact of the shelling was a thing that filled one's heart with terror. In the forests, tree bursts showered branches and splinters and sent trunks crashing into the snow. Rocket artillery, nicknamed "screaming meemies" for the sound they made when fired, was fired successively so that it rasped the already tense nerves of our green soldiers. By 6:15 a.m. the shelling finally stopped. Apparently, there were no direct hits scored because our medium (155mm) artillery battery was nestled in a valley. The 589th, 590th and 591st, which were the light (105mm) Field Artillery Battalions, received scattered hits. After the bombardment had stopped, it became quiet. It was an eerie quiet. This intense shelling was the beginning of *The Battle of the Bulge*.

Even while the shelling was going on, the kitchen personnel at our battery prepared a hot breakfast and served it around 7 a.m. while it was still dark. Battle procedure was in effect ever since we went into position on December 10th. Men did not cluster in groups and only a limited number of men approached the kitchen truck at a time to get their food in order to avoid being in a large concentration in case an artillery shell fell in our area.

Since it was my turn to be part of the group to go forward that morning to our Forward Observation (FO) post in Roth, Germany, our crew made ready for departure. At 8 a.m. our FO party mounted our two vehicles consisting of a Jeep and a ¼-ton Dodge truck (weapons carrier) with food, rations, our bedrolls and our carbines slung over our shoulders. The lead vehicle was the Jeep. Seated in the front seat of the Jeep was the Jeep driver, PFC Larry Loudon, and next time him was 1st Lt. Rex C. Matson, the Reconnaissance Officer (RO). I was seated in the rear seat of the Jeep.

The weapons carrier, which had a .50 caliber machine gun mounted at the rear of the cab, would follow the Jeep driven by PFC Terrill Rigdon. Seated next to Rigdon was T/4 Harold Hallberg, the radio operator. Seated in the rear of the weapons carrier were six telephone wiremen who's job it was to lay new telephone lines from the Observation Post in Roth to the gun position in Laudesfeld because the massive shelling knocked out our lines of communication. One of those wiremen assigned to this mission was PFC Howard Hoffmeyer, a good friend of mine. No military vehicles carrying personnel while in combat were allowed to have canvas tops on them regardless of the weather because they hindered observation and impeded quick vehicular exit in case of an enemy attack, as I would soon find out.

As we pulled away from our Battery's gun position, I said goodbye to my two close buddies, Carl Himberg and Bill Sewart. On the way to the front, we stopped at Divisional Headquarters to get the latest information about the frontlines as to where we were headed. Major Morgan, Intelligence Officer (G-2) for the 592nd Field Artillery Battalion told us that the early morning shelling was normal and that we should proceed to our mission at Roth. Obviously, Major Morgan didn't know any more than we did.

What Major Morgan and everyone else, including General Dwight D. Eisenhower's Supreme Headquarters Allied Expeditionary Forces (SHAEF), did not fully realize was that the German Army was in the process of launching a Counter-Offensive against the Allies. It came as a complete tactical surprise. The attack was dreamed up by Adolf Hitler and executed by Field Marshall Walter Von Model. The objective was to split the British and American Armies and overtake Antwerp, Belgium, which was a vital point for Allied supplies and the Germans desperately need it to carry on the war. In order to get there the Germans had to take St. Vith, Belgium with its five main highways and three rail lines. That was the first focal point of the attack and the 106th Infantry Division, newly arrived from the United States and only six days on the frontline, was placed squarely in the enemy's path. Von Model's timetable called for the capture of St. Vith within 24 hours.

The Ardennes region comprised of evergreen crested hills and narrow rivers between the steep banks winding through the thick woods. French General Charles Louis Marie Lanzerac called the Ardennes a "death trap." History has since revealed that the Allies knew about the German attack and that the SHAEF G-2 documents dated December 10, 1944 (the day our

Division went on the frontlines) dismissed the capabilities of the armored reserve to build up and attack. The wicked terrain was another reason the SHAEF Intelligence refused to believe a counter attack was possible. The winter season along with the ground covered with snow of up to six inches, and more in some places, would certainly impede vehicular movement.

The German Intelligence knew that the weakest point in the American Forces was the Ardennes-Eifel area, which was fortified by the newly arrived 106th Infantry Division. It was nearly impossible for the American Forces to observe what was going on in the German sector because of the fog and bad weather. The Allied Aerial reconnaissance was also nullified because of the weather. Even though our Air Force was superior to that of the Germans, it was inoperable.

The power of the German offensive was mighty. On the north was the Sixth SS Panzer Army. On the south was the Fifth SS Panzer Army. On the right, to the northern shoulder, was the German Fifteenth Army while on the left was the Seventh Army to the northern shoulder of the attack. In all, some twenty-two German Divisions were involved, ten of them Panzers. Of these Divisions poised for the attack, three of the Panzers Divisions were in the initial jump off.

The American Forces in defense of the initial attack of the affected area consisted of the 99th Infantry Division on the north, and the VIII Corps of the U.S. First Army on the right. The 106th Infantry Division with the 14th Cavalry group attached defended the left flank. South of the 106th Division were the 28th Infantry Division, the 9th Armored Division and the 4th Infantry Division.

One must understand that the Germans had been at war for a long time before this Counter-Offensive. In addition, the German Divisions displayed an awesome ability to survive shattering numbers of casualties and yet rebound within weeks, as long as a reasonable remnant of the officer cadre escaped to train the replacement troops. So high were the professional attainments of the German Army that a handful of German officers sufficed to accomplish apparent miracles of training and leadership. So capable were German officers in transforming individual soldiers into cohesive units that in the German Army the company developed a sufficient sense of comradeship and solidarity that makes an army an effective fighting force. This is the kind of army that was attacking us.

With this information as a background, what our small group of inexperienced artillerymen faced in the minutes, hours and days ahead during the initial German Counter-Offensive became very personal to us and it became a story of self-survival.

Alert, Medell, Belgium Sig C 65-4

Fighting in Woods, Henumont, Bel 65-8

106th Prisoners Mendell.Belg 65-1

Fighting.Rodt.Belgium Sig C 65-14

106th M7's Advance Luexembourg 65-9

Fighting Into St Vith.Bel Sig C 65-6

Above photos by 106th Division Signal Corps

S/Sgt. Jack Roberts, Pfc. Oscar Plante, Tech. Sgt. 4 Bill Ruona
Murrigen, Germany
February 1945

S/Sgt. Jack Roberts
Murrigen, Germany
February 1945

Chapter 17

Ambushed & Captured

On our way to the Forward Observation post in Roth, Germany, the two-vehicle convoy with eleven soldiers followed a route that took us about one mile south and through the position of the 106th Division's 589th Field Artillery Battalion located west of Roth and then passed through the village of Auw about two miles further east. The road we traveled was barely two lanes wide and was covered with snow.

As we continued toward Roth, we observed that many trees had been shattered and uprooted from the early morning artillery barrages. Huge black impact craters could be seen scattered throughout the snow-covered fields. No one in our vehicle said a word as we observed the scarred earth. As we neared Roth, we drove up a slight rise in the road through a section of the Ardennes Forest where snow covered trees lined both sides of the twisting road.

After rounding a bend in the road, we entered a small clearing when all hell broke loose. We were suddenly greeted by all kinds of small arms fire. We had driven directly into a German ambush! Crisscrossing fire from rifles and machine guns battered our two vehicles, with bullets whizzing by each one of us. We were like sitting ducks. Both drivers slammed on their brakes and the vehicles came to a skidding halt. Our Jeep driver, Larry Loudon, who was sitting directly in front of me, was immediately hit in the right arm. Before the Jeep came to a complete stop I had already jumped from it and dove into the ditch on the left side of the road. Larry and Lt. Matson scrambled out of the jeep and fell into the ditch on the right side of the road as the Jeep rolled to the edge of the road and turned over. The men from the weapons carrier also chose to seek shelter on the right side of the road, but were more exposed to the gunfire.

The soldier assigned as the machine gun operator in the weapons carrier was shot in the head before he could fire a single round and my good friend Cpl. Howard Hoffmeyer was instantly killed in the first volley of fire as he sat in his seat in the rear of the weapons carrier. These two soldiers were our first combat casualties, which gave us a shock of reality that we were at war. The war had now become a personal matter with us!

After jumping in the ditch, I immediately shouldered my carbine to fire at the enemy and raised my head only enough so I would not get it blown off. When I aimed my carbine at the movement in the short distance away in front of me, I was faced for the first time with killing another human being. My religious upbringing taught me "Thou Shalt Not Kill." I also remembered my Army training in preparation for going overseas where we were told to either "kill or be killed." I pulled off my gloves to get a better grip on my weapon. Even so, my finger was reluctant to pull the trigger, but I was a soldier and my training told me that I must fire my weapon at the enemy. It was also a survival decision. To kill a human was very traumatic for me as a tender young man of twenty years. After I fired the first round, the succeeding rounds were easier. I have often wondered if one of my bullets killed a German soldier, a human being. I don't know and it is just as well that I don't have the answer. The ambush and firing a weapon at the enemy for the first time was my "baptism of fire!"

Those of us who were physically able, fired our carbines at the enemy at the edge of the forest. I fired at anything that moved. The return fire from the Germans was horrific. We never realized it but we were facing the whole German Army and delaying its offensive by critical minutes toward its objective to take St. Vith, Belgium. We soon realized by the number of bullets whizzing around us that we were terribly outnumbered. This was not a patrol firing on us. We held our defensive position as long as we could. By this time a couple of the guys ran to my side of the road after I yelled to them that I had better protection from the German fire. One of the men to join me was Lt. Matson.

Apparently Lt. Matson thought in order to lead he must take the initiative. He started to stand up and I yelled at him to stay down or he would be killed. He said that somebody should get on the machine gun that was mounted on the back of the weapons carrier cab. I pleaded with him not to try it as bullets were flying every which way. He would be a visible target. He ignored me and as he stood up to reach the road a hail of gunfire lifted the earth around him and he came tumbling into the ditch next to me groaning in extreme pain. He had been hit in the arm. In addition to the two soldiers who were killed by this time, another seven of my comrades were seriously wounded from gunfire. The radio operator, Harold Hallberg, the weapons carrier driver, Terrill Rigdon, and me seemed to have survived the attack.

We held our position as long as we could. Those of our group who were wounded and could not fire their weapons reduced our firepower. Several of our group, when crossing the road to my side, got hit. Lt. Matson asked me what we should do. After surveying the hopelessness of our situation and as I looked at the hollow faces of our wounded and heard their mournful cries, I told Lt. Matson that I thought we should surrender or we would all be killed one way of another. Lt. Matson then gave me the order to surrender. That is when I reached into my pocket and pulled out a white handkerchief (which had been used several times) and tied it to the tip of the barrel of my carbine and began waiving it back and forth. Just that quickly, the firing stopped and about twenty screaming German soldiers dressed in white camouflage suits with white helmets came rushing toward us carrying automatic pistols and rifles that were painted white.

From the way the German soldiers were carrying on, it seemed as though they either could taste victory or they were high on some kind of drug. Only the men in our group who were physically able to raise their arms lifted them to surrender. Suddenly we were surrounded by a handful of German soldiers as the remainder of the Germans ran past us and continued down the road toward the village of Auw. Quickly, the German soldiers confiscated our weapons and took everything out of our pockets of a personal nature, including the Waltham wristwatch that I was wearing. One thing they failed to find on me was a crucifix deep in my pants pocket that I carried the entire time I was in the service and used it frequently in prayer. In so doing, the Germans physically jerked us around in spite of the wounds that my comrades suffered.

We were unable to understand what the Germans were screaming at us. One of the Germans started to take the dog tags off one of our dead comrades. I would guess that he wanted them as a souvenir. I protested by foolishly grabbing the German and with that he screamed at me with wild eyes and poked his "burp" gun (automatic pistol) so deep into my left gut area that I thought the barrel would come out my backside. I thought for sure he was going to kill me. Had I had an opportunity to look at my body later on I know I would have seen severe bruise marks. I am thankful I did what I did because the German did not remove the dog tags from either of our two dead soldiers.

Looking back on the ambush, I feel quite confident that the ambush that our small group encountered so early on the first morning of the German Army's drive delayed them for critical minutes, which worked against its timetable to meet its goal to take St. Vith within the first 24 hours. In spite of being captured, following the ambush, I feel satisfied that our group's defensive action made a contribution to the eventual success in defeating the enemy.

Our ambush was officially document by Lt. Col. Richard E. Weber, Battalion Commander 592nd Field Artillery Battalion in his After Action Report for the period 10-16 December 1944 and currently recorded in the Adjutant General's Office, Washington, DC, which stats:

> 1st Lieutenant Rex C. Matson, RO of Battery "C", and his party were ambushed while they were going to their observation post at Roth. This news reached Captain Robert W. Smith, Commanding Officer, Battery "C" in the afternoon while he was returning from the rear echelon.

Chapter 18

A Prisoner of War

After stripping us of our personal possessions, two of the German soldiers dressed in white ordered us to start walking and pointed toward a section of the dense forest. Our wounded helped each other and I assigned myself to Larry Loudon, my Jeep driver and a good friend of mine, since he was one of the more severely wounded. Because he was losing a lot of blood, I half carried him to keep him on his feet.

As we stumbled into the forest, we found ourselves in the midst of a German command post. The nine of us stood in a clustered group for a short time waiting for further action against us. While waiting to see what their next move would be, I noticed that there were many German soldiers and officers poised for advance toward the Americans along with equipment including tanks, antitank vehicles, machine guns, cannons and other vehicles. Other German officers were barking orders and looking at maps that were spread out on the hoods of vehicles and hung from tree trunks.

The stench of fuel, engine exhaust and gun powder, mixed with the cold air, the loud noise of motors and the clattering of tank treads confined within the forest was frightening. Overhead we could hear artillery shells being fired toward the American positions. I made up my mind that I would get the hell out of that situation at the first chance I got.

We were then handed over to two German soldiers dressed in regular uniforms. They became our guards. They nudged us along with their guns and gave us some German command to begin walking, thereby marching us off behind the lines and deeper into German-held territory. At this point it looked as if the war was over for my fellow soldiers and me. It bothered me to no end that we had to leave our dead comrades behind. Those of us who could walk continued to help each other. I continued to help my buddy Larry Loudon because he could barely walk. The loss of blood from being wounded and the pain in his arm were beginning to have an effect on his mobility.

Reality struck me all at once. I, along with my fellow soldiers, had just become a Prisoner of War with no means of escape and I had to do what I was ordered to do by the enemy. As we slowly trudged through a field where the snow was as deep as a foot in some areas, none of us said a word. The wounded were in great pain. The fact that there was no medical attention or first aid, and no signs of when they would get any in the immediate future had to be very physically and mentally traumatic for them. I had absolutely no idea of what time of the day it was because I didn't have a watch and the skies were dark gray.

I would learn much later what was happening to us at this time. The German 290th Regiment of the 18th Volksgrenadier Division (VGD) had ambushed us and later overran our Battery position. The objective of the 18th VGD was to get to St. Vith, Belgium and during its approach it handed the U.S. Army one of its worst defeats in history. Notably, two regiments of the 106th Infantry Division, the 422nd and 423rd, were surrounded and also captured, but not without a great fight.

I knew that something terrible was happening and I was very concerned that our Battery Commander, Captain Robert W. Smith, had no knowledge as to what was happening and there was no way we could communicate with him. As a twenty-year old kid, I was scared and I felt sure my fellow soldiers were just as scared. Surrendering to the enemy is something you don't train for before going overseas.

As we pushed through the snow, my mind was running wild with all kinds of thoughts. I thought about my fiancée, my parents and my brother. *Would they ever learn my fate and if so, when? Are these two German guards under "take no prisoners" orders, and were they taking us out in the field to kill us?* Not knowing our fate, I was mentally devastated. All we could do was walk, hope and pray, and I surely did my share of praying.

The war was over at this point for the nine of us, but the war for the rest of the Division was just beginning. I would later learn that when the 592nd Field Artillery Battalion received the news about the massive German offensive headed their way, they began continuously firing all three Batteries (A, B and C), which consisted of twelve howitzers. They began to run short of ammunition because the ammunition train (trucks loaded with artillery shells) had gotten no farther than the village of Schoenberg, Germany when they were stopped.

The 589th and 592nd Battalions were in a hot spot. The enemy got so close to the gun positions that the howitzers fired point blank against tanks advancing from the village of Auw. Divisional Artillery headquarters ordered the 589th and 592nd to withdraw to a rearward position. The guys at C/592 worked feverishly all night on December 16th trying to get the 155mm howitzers hooked up to the Caterpillar tractors (referred to as CATs), which had become mired in the mud. In so doing, Lt. Kennedy from C-Battery lost the tip of his finger. Both A/589 and C/592 each lost one howitzer early in the battle.

It was a race against time to get the guns out before being overrun by the Germans. C/592 was able to make its withdrawal just in time. However, before pulling out, C/592 lost its Forward Observer at the command post in Roth and its Reconnaissance Officer, Lt. Matson, in the ambush, so the Battery's Executive Officer, Lt. Al Siekierski, had to assume the duties of Forward Observer in addition to his duties as XO. At one point, he stood on a pile of live ammunition with a pair of field glasses and managed to place several volleys of fire from two of the Battery's howitzers on the village of Auw by adjusting the range from the Church steeple. He was able to disrupt the enemy columns that were pressing forward on the important strategic road to the town of St. Vith.

Perhaps the 106th Infantry Division was a "green" Division with many of its soldiers being inadequately trained. However, it is interesting to note that the 18th VGD had gained almost two months experience in the Eifel since they had arrived from southern Denmark in November 1944. As a German Reserve Division, the officer corps was young and the majority lacked combat experience. A small cadre of experienced soldiers transformed the Division into a fighting unit. One of them was Lieutenant Hans Joachim Neutmann, the adjutant for II Battalion,

295th Grenadier-Regiment. He was a career soldier who joined the Wehmacht at the age of seventeen in 1941 and served extensively on the Eastern Front. Three-fourths of the rank and file consisted of fillers who had no combat experience. The inexperienced came from former Luftwaffe Field Divisions, the Kriegsmarine (German Navy), or were young recruits or ethnic Germans who lived outside Germany's immediate boundaries. In many respects, these were two green Divisions facing each other.

The nine of us prisoners from C/592 continued our march from the German command post under the watchful eye of our newly assigned guards. Later, I learned that we were being marched toward the Belgium border from Germany, north by northwest. We walked slowly because of the pace of our wounded comrades. The deep snow also slowed us down. The German guards enticed us to walk faster by prodding us with their weapons, yelling German commands, and pointing their guns at us as if they were going to shoot us.

Trudging through deep snow was not easy for me, especially since my nerves were tense and I carried the weight of my wounded comrade. By this time, I had as much of Larry's blood on me as he had on his own clothing.

We walked down a hillside and at the bottom we reached a creek that was frozen over with a coating of ice. (Years later, I learned that the creek was named Tennenbach Creek.) The guards as well as my seven comrades all walked over the ice without incident. To add more misery to a deplorable situation for Larry Loudon and myself, as I was supporting him across the ice, just as we neared the other side of the frozen creek, the ice broke and we both fell into the ice-cold stream up to our knees. Water rushed inside our combat boots and our legs, hands and arms were soaking wet from where we had kept ourselves from falling bodily into the stream. I had to generate a lot of energy to pull the two of us out onto the bank of the creek. Walking in deep snow in the dead of winter with the cold wind biting you in the face and wet clothing does not improve one's morale. When our German guards saw what happened to Larry and me, they both laughed at us. I already began to dread what was going to happen to my feet during the next hours, days and months ahead, because I knew that there was no dry clothing to look forward to.

We continued our march deeper into German territory. Larry was becoming weaker the further we walked—the loss of blood was taking its toll. Larry was using up my strength, but he would have done the same thing for me. Soldiers are brothers who will do anything to help each other out. He kept trying to pass out on me but I would not let him for fear that the Germans would either shoot him or let him lie in the snow covered field and die from exposure due to the severe cold weather.

During our march we periodically had to throw ourselves to the ground when we heard artillery shells screaming in for a hit nearby. When an artillery shell explodes, fragments from the explosion spread over a wide area so the danger of being wounded exists within the vicinity. I had no idea whether the shells were from the Germans or the Americans. When we did not get up off the ground soon enough after the shelling, the German guards would use the barrel of their guns to prod our bodies to hurry us along. Throughout our march, my wounded comrades kept moaning and grieving with pain as the Germans just laughed and hollered at us. We had no idea what they were saying. Many hours had passed and the wounded still had not received any needed medical attention. When we did not move fast enough for our German Guards, they again raised their weapons and aimed them at us and acted like they were going to kill us. I admit we cringed with fear, which also made our guards laugh at us. Several times I thought their actions were orders from their commander to take us to a remote area to kill us. This gesture on their part not only scared me but it was also very humiliating.

Later, our German guards herded us toward a cow path between two hedgerows that led toward a small village. I learned years later that the village was named Weckerath and was located in Germany.

Unknown to our German guards, inside Weckerath were the remnants of Troop "C" of the 14th Cavalry who were defending the village against the Germans. We followed the cow path a short distance. For some reason, Larry and I were in the lead of our group. Just as we rounded a bend that led into the village ahead of us, an American tank appeared crossing our path at the end of the lane. (I learned later that the tank was from Troop "F" of the 18th Cavalry, which was just arriving in the village to rescue Troop "C" of the 14th Cavalry.) At the exact moment that I saw the tank, the tank's turret gunner looked down our way and saw us. I immediately hollered to our guys, "Hit the dirt!" in order to give the turret gunner a clear shot at the two Germans who were guarding us. Since the Germans did not understand English, they did not know what I said so they were standing exposed to the turret gunner. To our misfortune, the tank driver had no idea what was happening and by the time the turret gunner turned his machine gun in our direction the tank continued on its path into the village of Weckerath. The turret gunner was not able to shoot over our heads at the two German soldiers.

By the grace of God, at that precise moment the tank commander was walking behind his tank and saw us hit the ground with the two Germans standing over us. He immediately recognized our plight and, with his "Tommy gun," gave chase after the Germans when they turned and ran back down the cow path. I would learn many years later that the soldier who killed one of the German guards was S/Sgt. John J. Keogh from F-Troop, 18th Cavalry. The second guard escaped. For his heroic action he was awarded the Silver Star medal for rescuing my comrades and me.

We used this surprising and welcome turn of events to pick ourselves up from the ground. I helped Larry to his feet and our group then followed the path of the tank deeper into the village, which was now under artillery fire. The farmhouses and barns were being destroyed, and fires were starting around the village. My comrades and I escaped our German captors but we were not yet free, as we would soon learn. We found the command post and met the Commander of Troop "C" of the 14th Cavalry. I learned many years later that his name was Captain John T. Walker. Captain Walker was surprised to see our group and wanted to know where we came from. We quickly told him about being ambushed and captured and how we eventually escaped at the outskirts of the village. He was sympathetic with our capture and impressed with our survival, but he offered us no comfort. He then told us that the village was being surrounded by the Germans and had become a target for their artillery and that we would have to fight our way out for survival to avoid being killed or captured.

We told Captain Walker that most of our group had been wounded in the ambush except Hallberg, Rigdon and me. That is when Captain Walker questioned me about the blood on my clothes. I assured him that I was not wounded and that the blood came from carrying my buddy who got hit in the arm in the ambush.

Captain Walker then gave Hallberg a .45 caliber pistol and gave an M-1 rifle to Rigdon. Rigdon had been slightly wounded in the ambush but at the time did not realize it. The Captain then looked at me and said that the only weapon he could give me were hand grenades. I shoved four of them into my coat pockets. At this point my arms, hands, legs and feet were extremely cold and numb. Frankly, I did not feel any pain because my body had adjusted to the cold and my mind was too preoccupied with survival to care about any pain or discomfort. Our next challenge was to get out of Weckerath alive.

Chapter 19

The Escape

Time was running out. By this time the Germans blocking our escape route had surrounded the village of Weckerath and the thunderous volleys from the German artillery were blowing up the village. Captain Walker ordered all personnel consisting of those soldiers from his Troop along with our artillery group and me, into the center of the village. He then ordered whatever vehicles were operable onto the main road where we were waiting. This was an area somewhat protected from the view of the Germans. Captain Walker told everyone that we would attempt to make our escape in two waves. The first wave would consist of all the wounded who would be loaded into the heavily armored vehicles. The remaining soldiers would then follow in whatever vehicles remained using the same escape route as the first wave.

I was part of the second wave. I mounted the back of a 2 ½-ton GMC truck with several other soldiers where we laid flat on our backs on the steel bed of the truck. As I laid on my back, I continued to hear the German artillery shells crashing in the village and exploding. The dense smoke from the fires was billowing all over the village and I watched the tops of wooden telephone poles burning.

The first wave left the village of Weckerath, located inside the German border, and headed toward the village of Manderfeld, which was about a mile northeast and just over the Belgium border. The village of Manderfeld held the headquarters of Troop "C" of the 14th Cavalry and also housed a field First Aid station. If we made it out of the village our wounded would be able to get some extremely necessary medical treatment.

When it came time for the second wave to leave Weckerath, the driver of the truck I was in revved up the engine and shifted gears as fast as he could. He was going fairly fast by the time he hit the outskirts of the village and got out in the open. That is when we ran the gauntlet through the German's small arms crossfire. Lying on my back, I could see the bullets splintering the wooden seat back slats on the back of the truck just over my head.

As the truck bounced along I couldn't help but think about what would happen if the truck driver got shot or if a tire got blown out. The road to Manderfeld was nothing more than a single lane cow path covered with snow. If we slid off the road for whatever reason the truck would most certainly overturn and the soldiers inside would fall out and perhaps be killed in the wreckage. If not, we would be injured or worse yet the pins in the hand grenades in my pockets would fall out and I would be blown to bits. Should I survive such an accident, I would be captured again. Being captured once was enough and I did not like the idea of being taken a prisoner a second time.

These thoughts were not very comforting, but such things do race through the mind under such circumstances. I prayed also. The Lord had taken care of me so far and I asked Him to help me escape once again. One fears the unknown.

The truck I was in was the second to last vehicle and the last vehicle to leave the village was the Jeep containing Captain Walker and his driver. How he survived running the gauntlet in an open Jeep is another miracle.

During my research for information about the 14th Cavalry, I learned that the Captain who masterminded our escape was Captain John T. Walker. It was at this time that I also learned that the last vehicle had no more than left Weckerath when the full force of the German artillery leveled the village. We got out just in time. I owe my life to two Cavalrymen—S/Sgt. John J. Keogh and Captain John T. Walker—and to the good Lord.

With the grace of God and prayer, the truck I was in survived the crossfire gauntlet and arrived in the village of Manderfield, and the headquarters of the 14th Cavalry and the First Aid Station. When I crawled from the back of the 2 ½-ton GMC, I looked at the truck. It looked like Swiss cheese with all the bullet holes in it. It was truly a miracle that we made it out alive and just in time.

I had no knowledge if any of the other vehicles made the escape, but I felt confident that the heavier armored vehicles containing our wounded survived the ambush. I began to search the various rooms of the First Aid buildings for Larry as well as my other wounded comrades, but was unable to find any of them. However, I did find both Harold Hallberg and Terrill Rigdon.

I knew from my horrible experiences that day on December 16, 1944 that I did not want to be taken prisoner again. Nor did I want to join the 14th Cavalry, even though they were responsible for saving my life as well as my fellow soldiers more than once. I did not belong with the 14th Cavalry. I needed to get back to Battery "C," 592nd Field Artillery Battalion where I belonged.

Hallberg and Rigdon asked me what we should do. I told them that I was not about to be taken prisoner again if I could help it and that I was going to try to find my way back to our Battery. They wanted to know how I was going to do that. I told them I had no idea except to start out towards the American frontlines. But first I was going to need a compass and then strike out on my own toward the west to take my chances. I told them that they could stay with the 14th Cavalry or they could join me in my escape. Both of them chose to go with me. I felt we had nothing to lose. I needed a compass because we would be traveling in the dark of night and under cloudy gray skies during the daylight hours with no visible means of direction.

After several attempts to find someone who had a compass, I finally found a Cavalry Lieutenant who gave one to me when I told him our plight. With the "gift" he said, "Good luck soldier." I had no intentions of being a hero. I was just a young kid who was scared, cold and too dumb to know any different. I just wanted to get back to my own outfit.

By this time darkness had settled in. At that time of the year in Belgium and Germany darkness began to fall at about 4:45 p.m. It was later than that but it was time to make our move because we were told that the Germans were moving from Weckerath to Manderfeld in order to surround it. We walked between several buildings and then to the edge of a field. I looked at my compass to find where the west was located.

Knowing what we experienced in Weckerath when the Germans poured in its artillery shells, I certainly did not want to take the chance of being killed by artillery if I remained in Manderfeld.

My feet were so cold and numb along with my hands that I barely felt any pain. I had taken my gloves off to fire my carbine at the Germans during the ambush when we surrendered to the enemy and my gloves remained laying in the snow. I sure could have used them at this point.

Without food, water or warm clothing, the three of us then slipped out of Manderfeld and cautiously sneaked through the darkness and the Germans surrounding the village. We began our long trek heading west using the compass as our guide to find the American forces. We were constantly on the alert and always fearful of stepping on a land mine that might have been planted by the Germans during their defensive position when being pushed back by the Americans earlier in the war.

We kept a low profile to avoid being hit by sniper fire; we knew our dark clothing against the white snow was surely a way for us to be detected. We rarely talked, except in low tones, and we distanced ourselves from each other so all three of us could not be killed at one time by a mortar or artillery shell being lobbed in, which were many. Because we didn't know exactly where we were going, the shelling could have come from either the Germans or the Americans.

The sound of small arms fire and artillery remained constant. At night the sound is even more eerie because of the flashes of light from either the large guns firing or the exploding of shells when they strike the ground. The German Counter-Offensive was now in full force. The German Army was in front of us invading the American frontlines and pushing them further back into Belgium but we did not know at what speed this was happening. We knew it was necessary for us to move with the Germans because we had to travel with them in order to eventually get through their frontlines to find the American frontlines. This would not be an easy task—it was quite dangerous. We pondered our fate constantly, but kept moving ever so cautiously.

We traveled mostly in the wooded areas of the Ardennes as well as the lowlands to keep from being an easy target. We also kept off the roads and open fields as much as possible. Thank God for the Ardennes with its many trees. We did take time out to rest occasionally. We ate snow to keep from becoming dehydrated.

Sometime during the wee hours of the morning rain and then sleet began to fall. We came across a barn on the outskirts of a small village. (I learned much later that the name of the village was Eimerscheid). The barn looked inviting and it was a chance to get out of the sleet, wind and rain. We entered the barn ever so suspiciously. Here was an opportunity to get out of the elements so we climbed up a crude wooden ladder into the hayloft and snuggled under the hay to get some needed rest. We promptly went to sleep. Our nerves were frazzled at this point.

We didn't sleep very long because just before daybreak we could hear voices approaching the barn. Several people entered the barn and were speaking German. We could not see them from the hayloft, they could have been local farmers, but we felt they were German soldiers that stopped in the barn to get out of the beastly weather. We heard them laugh and talk and then they moved out. I wondered what we would do if they decided to get some rest in the hayloft as we were doing. I pulled one of the hand grenades out of my pocket and hooked my finger in the pin ready to pull it out and toss the grenade down from the loft to the floor of the barn if they started up the ladder. Hallberg and Rigdon had the rifle and pistol and I had no idea what they would do. Shortly, they left and I got a glimpse of the three, who were German soldiers. What a relief it was when they moved on. When we knew they were gone we resumed our trek once again. We were aware that whenever we stopped moving we lost precious time and distance in finding the Americans.

It was daylight when we left the barn. That is when Rigdon stopped and asked me to look at his neck. He said it had been bothering and hurting him. I looked at his neck where he pointed and I could see a long, red streak where a bullet had gone through his outer clothing and just grazed his neck and drew a little blood. The flesh was also burned from the friction of the bullet when it passed through his clothes and grazed his neck. He had a close call.

We were extremely careful and with the grace of God we continued our trek for the next couple of days. We traveled by day and night and every time we had to cross a road we crossed it one person at a time so if one of us got hit the other two would have a chance to get away. Running across an open road made us easy targets for the Germans if they saw us.

We had no nourishment with us. We didn't have "C" or "K" rations or even a candy bar to share. Only snow. I credit our early basic and advanced training for our survival, in addition to the good Lord who gave us the wisdom to use that training properly. During our trek across German held territory we were fired on from a distance several times but we were not hit. We were able to run into the forest where we kept running for a while before we stopped.

During our trek to find the Americans, we were constantly aware of our own vulnerability. We saw the movement of German troops, mechanization and weapons, but we always managed to keep our distance from them. What was really sickening and heartbreaking was to see the dead soldiers—both the Americans and the Germans, lying in the white snow, in pools of discolored red blood. Some soldiers were missing limbs and others certainly could not be recognizable except for their dog tags, when found and picked up by Graves Registration personnel. Many of the soldiers lying in the cold, red tainted white snow were in grotesque positions. I remember seeing one American soldier lying on his back with his eyes wide open looking through the gray colored sky toward heaven. I remember saying to myself, "My God. What on earth could he want to see even after death!" As Plato once said, "Only the dead have seen the end of war."

Since I did not have a defensive weapon, except my hand grenades, I picked up a "Tommy Gun" (Thompson Submachine Gun) and extra clips of ammunition lying near one of the dead American soldiers. I felt a little more secure with this weapon, should I need it.

There were also German and American vehicles that littered the roads. Deep artillery shell craters were everywhere. Many trees in parts of the forest were stripped of their limbs from artillery tree bursts and other very eerie sights to behold, but we kept moving since we were still behind enemy lines.

During the night we saw the V-1 and V-2 rockets, also known as buzz bombs, streaking overhead with the constant loud vibrating chatter of the jet engines. The rockets were being launched from launch pads further inside Germany. It was a sound that shattered our nerves almost to the breaking point. The roar of the jet engines left a white fire trail behind them that eventually disappeared in the low hanging clouds. The rockets launched behind German lines were electronically controlled and timed with its bomb built in the nose of the rocket. When the noise stopped, it meant that the engine shut down and the rocket dropped. Then the sky lit up, followed by the sound of a violent explosion. It sent chills down my spine. The V-1 rocket was designed for short-range targets while the V-2 was designed for long-range targets. We knew that when the engines stopped, it meant that the bomb would fall from the sky onto a target and crash to the earth with a tremendous explosion.

We were still lost, still alone, and still had no leadership except ourselves and we had no idea where we were or exactly where we were going. We did know that soon after leaving the village of Manderfeld we were traveling in Belgium. We were just trying to survive minute-by-minute, hour-by-hour and day-by-day. Being without food really never entered our minds. I guess we were hungry but we were too busy to think about food. Our survival depended on our wits at this point and not our stomachs.

None of us had a watch. We just guessed at the time and never thought much about what day it was. We had a goal to attain and that took up our strength, ingenuity and determination. We knew that the Americans were out there somewhere.

After several days of playing cat and mouse with the Germans behind their frontlines we felt we were getting closer to the American frontlines. We soon learned ways of knowing this because of troop and mechanization movements, the sound of artillery and our gut feeling.

Chapter 20

Freedom At Last

Our path to potential freedom occurred one morning shortly before dawn. As we were slipping across a small clearing the Germans fired yellow flares that parachuted slowly to the ground, which lit up a large area. Such flares always caused us to drop to the ground and lay motionless until the flares burned out. This particular shower of flares that morning gave us enough light to see in the distance the silhouette of what appeared to be an American tank. During basic and advanced training we had to identify all kinds of military vehicles both friendly as well as enemy. Now this training was again being tested. We were positive that the tank we were looking at was American because of its shape. When the flares burned out we advanced closer to the tank to make sure we finally achieved our objective and our pathway to freedom. Up until this point we were still escaped Prisoners of War in enemy territory.

It was still dark and we cautiously approached the tank's position. The noise from weapons being fired was deafening. We had to be careful when approaching the American lines so that we would not be shot. We learned several days earlier when we first took our positions on the frontline that Germans were known to masquerade as American soldiers and infiltrate or parachute behind American lines to cause havoc. We certainly did not want to get shot by our own American troops after going through what we did in the past several days.

All frontline troops were aware of this stolen identify breach. Such an incident faced a good friend of mine, the late Lt. Col. Thomas Dailey, who at that time was a Major when he had his own identity tested. He was with the 7th Armored in the area of St. Vith when this occurred. Major Dailey's unit had been designated as the Divisional reserve and was called up to go into action near St. Vith. En route to their position Tom was leading a column of tanks when he was forced to stop as a result of mines that had been placed in the road. Two American Military Police

(MPs) challenged him and wanted to see his identification. Tom was "pissed" and demanded an explanation. The MPs then told Major Dailey that German paratroopers had jumped behind the American lines disguised as American soldiers. The MPs proceeded to ask Tom questions that only a true American would know. Tom said he answered all of their questions and he said it was fortunate that he knew baseball as well as he did because one of the questions asked was for him to name the wife of the Brooklyn Dodgers manager, which he did.

Knowing that other soldiers and units were fighting their own wars, my two escapee comrades and I continued with our own war also. When the opportunity seemed right the three of us sneaked near the tank's position and proceeded to blend in with the action when we came across an American Sergeant. What a wonderful feeling it was to see another American and be with them once again. We made it. We were no longer escaped Prisoners of War, nor Missing in Action. In just six days I had personally been ambushed by the Germans, taken prisoner, fell into ice water and got my feet, legs, arms and hands wet, escaped the Germans at the village of Weckerath with the help of the 14th and 18th Cavalry units, was surrounded by the Germans while in Weckerath, escaped the village in an ambush through a hail of bullets and was able to escape from the village of Manderfeld after it was surrounded.

I also survived the long trek across Belgium exposed to horrible weather conditions without food or water and very little rest as we sneaked through the German frontlines without being shot or taken prisoner again. The three of us were indeed fortunate to have been through so much and yet survived one tragedy after the other. To live to be able to tell about it is truly a miracle. The hand of God had to be with us all the way.

When we approached the Sergeant he was quite surprised and immediately asked, "Who in the hell are you?" and we quickly told him we were from the 106th Infantry Division and had been captured by the Germans several days before but escaped and just now were able to get back to the American frontlines. He was not very interested so he referred us to his superior officer. We then told the Lieutenant our story and that we wanted to find our battery in the 106th Division. He had no idea where our Division was located and pointed us in a direction which he thought we might be able to find a command post that might be able to give us the location of our Division.

We would soon learn that the frontlines were in total disarray and confusion. No one was sure where their own units were fighting let alone know were any other outfits were located. It was a fight for survival for both unit and individual.

While we were traveling to survive as individuals so was the 106th Infantry Division. The Division had already lost its 422nd and 423rd Infantry Regiments in addition to parts of other units, such as the 81st Engineers, the 589th, 590th and 591st Field Artillery Battalions. In one case in particular another good friend of mine, Captain James Fonda, Battery Commander of Battery "B", 590th FA Battalion, had to surrender his entire battery because it was surrounded by the Germans but not before destroying their four 105mm howitzers.

Attached to the 106th, the 7th Armored Division began arriving on December 17th. For those of the 106th who were holding the thin lines and faced the bitter cold under bone chilling conditions, the thought of combat was the furthest from their minds. Thoughts of a warm Christmas at home were the furthermost from reality. The conditions were such that water froze almost instantly and even spoken words seemed to hang in the air.

Little did the defenders realize that on December 17th, the second day of the German Counter-Offensive, the full weight of the German Army had descended upon their positions during the early morning. Fighting a war is hellish enough in good weather but to fight a war in such miserable conditions tested the strength of each soldier on the frontlines for the Allies as well as the Germans.

Brigadier General Bruce Clarke arrived in St. Vith at 10:30 a.m. on the 17th. According to Capt. Woodruff of the 106th Division Headquarters who's own headquarters was located in a school house, said that the situation was rather chaotic with all the Divisional Headquarters Personnel abandoning the buildings. Hearing sounds of small arms fire and looking out, Woodruff could see German troops off in the distance moving against American positions. About that time is when Major General Alan W. Jones, the commanding officer of the 106th Division, reported that two of his regiments, the 422nd and 423rd, were cut off in the region of the Schnee-Eifel. The Eifel was located east and southeast of Schoenberg, and the remaining regiment, the 424th, had been badly hit by German troops and had occupied Heuen, located between St. Vith and Schoenberg.

All of this was just part of the fierce battles that were taking place within the twenty-five-mile front that the 106th was covering when the German Counter-Offensive began on December 16, 1944.

By this time, dawn was breaking still under dark gray clouds and not having any idea what was going on at that time, the three of us blindly began to again strike out on our own looking for the command post that just might give us some idea as to where we were and where we might be able to find C/592. At least our search would now be behind the American frontlines and not behind the enemy's frontlines.

Chapter 21

Searching for the 592nd

The next three days (December 19, 20, and 21) were rather hectic. We traveled in and around the American lines with many different units trying to find our 592nd Artillery unit. The confusion at that time was almost disastrous. I cannot remember the units we were with but they ranged from Armored units, to Infantry, to Cavalry, to Artillery. Those with whom we made contact in each unit tried to be helpful but were thoroughly confused themselves. Nevertheless, I will give a synopsis of just some of the highlights I can remember that we experienced during those three grueling days.

Shortly after leaving the tank unit, we ran into an Infantry Captain. We asked him where our unit, the 592nd, would be. He showed us the general area on the map and pointed to the road we should follow.

This was a grand and glorious feeling to be able to mix with American forces once again. Although we were not out of danger, we felt good about being back among the Americans.

We started down the road the Captain showed us and after walking for a while we came to a fork in the road. Without a map we were unsure as to which of the two roads to take so we chose one. Unfortunately we chose to take the road that led toward a German emplacement.

As we were walking down the road we heard a plane overhead and noticed it was an American P-47 Thunderbolt fighter plane. The plane made several passes and then all at once turned back toward the direction we were walking in and came roaring down the road. As the plane neared us the pilot fired his six .50 caliber machine guns over our heads. Some form of enemy target was in the direction we were traveling in. The plane's actions caused us to dive into a ditch. Then we watched as the plane strafed some Germans as they fired back at the plane. Had it not been for the P-47, we might have walked right into another German ambush.

We crawled out of the ditch and as soon as we got back onto the road we ran back to the fork in the road so we could take the other road. However, we were all a little uptight because now we wondered what we might find going down the other road which could be equally as hazardous.

Bounding down the other road, we found some infantrymen who were fighting. The lieutenant welcomed us and said that the German advance was driving the Americans back into Belgium. The news that the Americans lacked air support due to bad weather and no additional troops arriving did not raise our morale.

The lieutenant did give us a ride and everywhere we stopped we asked about our unit. At one of the stops a Captain offered to help us and I rode with him to find the location of the 592nd Field Artillery unit. My trek with him turned out to be another grueling experience.

This Captain had no regard for danger. While we rode along I began to wonder if he cared whether he lived or died. He was doing me a favor by stopping wherever there was activity and asking questions as to where my outfit might be. However, we were fired at by German small arms fire and shells fell too close for comfort.

We finally reached the Captain's superior and I told him my story and asked him where the 592nd could be. He was quite impressed with our escape and was concerned about the blood on my clothes and I had to assure him that I was not wounded. He then gave me a new lead as to where we might find the 592nd, which was still active and fighting. He said the 592nd was somewhere in a southerly direction in the vicinity of St. Vith, Belgium.

With that bit of good news, I returned back to Hallberg and Rigdon. Much to my pleasure I learned that they got their first meal. When the Captain asked me if I was hungry I told him I was but did not want to take any time out to eat, but I did accept a couple boxes of "K" rations. These "K" rations were the first food I had since breakfast on December 16th. I had never tasted anything so good in all my life. Food was in short supply for the troops since the supply trains could not get through.

After thanking the captain for his help and the other soldiers for the food, we began to walk down the road when a 2 ½-ton truck drove by. We flagged it down to give us a ride. The driver was headed for ammunition and we could ride in the back of his truck. I still had my compass and as long as we headed west, I was satisfied.

After riding a short while, the driver told us that this was the end of the line. We thanked him and headed on our way. By this time it was late in the day and we could still hear and see the V-1 bombs flying overhead.

We found ourselves in a small village where the headquarters for an outfit was located. They offered us a place to sleep for the night. Since we had no bedrolls or any personal gear with us, we huddled in the back of a truck that had a canvas over the top to keep out the cold wind. My feet continued to remain frozen and totally numb. We catnapped through the night to the sounds of artillery barrages. The war continued to go on around us.

We had the same experience this day as in the past few days. It was a hit or miss trek looking for our unit. We headed in the general direction of St. Vith that day, walking and hitching a couple of short rides. Someone told us that he heard that the 592nd was still in existence, although somewhat crippled, but they were still delivering their fire missions. This made us feel pretty good. It was as if we had a home to go to for sure.

The noises were forever prevalent. The creaking tank treads, engines of all kinds, and the firing of weapons formed a collective sound all its own. There is a decisive odor that is also present. The combination of gunpowder, exhaust, and fuel fumes mixed with the cold, damp air is nauseating. There is no way that such sounds and smells could be repeated in any form other than that of the combat zone. We continued to stare into the face of our own mortality as we traveled to find our unit.

That night we holed up in a small village. Here we found a Cavalry unit and were told that we could spend the night there. There were no extra blankets or bedrolls, but inside the house seemed like paradise even though it was cold and damp. Having seen so many building get shelled within the past few days, I had the subconscious feeling that again we may be the targets of an enemy artillery shell. But my fears were unfounded. Fortunately, that night went rather well.

Having lost track of time we just lived from one day to the next. Not having a bath for several weeks was beginning to tell on me. My skin was so dry and flaky and I was starting to itch.

Around daybreak, we decided to leave the Cavalry unit. A telephone lineman at the Calvary unit was on a field telephone as we started to leave so I asked him if he could call his switchboard and see if there might be someone at headquarters who might know the location of our unit. As he made the call we stood by. Within minutes the field phone rang and it was his headquarters. He said that our unit was heard to be in the vicinity of Vielsalm, Belgium. We thanked him and started on our way once again. Luckily, it turned out to be a very good lead.

After hitching a few rides with different outfits, late in the day we ran across a Corps artillery unit. A lieutenant told us to stay with his unit until he could pin point the exact location. He said he would see that we were reunited with out battery the next day. We knew now that we were close. The officer told us that we should get a hot meal as it was then evening chow time. We were famished and it really tasted good. This was my first hot meal in five days.

The next morning, December 21st, a Sergeant came to us where we bedded down for the night, which was in the back of a truck. He said that he had more news for us as the 592nd was suppose to be at Rosee, fifteen miles west of Dinant.

I would later learn that our Divisional Artillery had pushed for Erizee and the 592nd rolled through Lierneux and at last, a half mile from Vielsalm. It was at 7:30 p.m. on the night of December 20th when our unit went into position near Commanster to reinforce the 591st Field Artillery Battalion. Commanster became our destination for the day. Here is where we hoped we would find Battery C, after being gone for five days.

From the time we made our escape at Manderfeld to Commanster, I would estimate the distance to be about twenty-five miles in a straight line, but on foot and zigzagging throughout the five days meant that we traveled many more miles than that.

We arrived at the gun position at around noon. The first person we ran into was our Battery Commander, Captain Smith. I rarely saw him smile, but when he saw us he grinned from ear to ear and welcomed us back. Up until that moment he thought we had been killed, captured, or wounded because all he heard about our whereabouts was that we had been ambushed on our way to Roth.

Since he saw the blood on my uniform, he asked me was if I was wounded. I explained that the blood belonged to Larry Loudon and briefly explained our ordeal during the past six days. I told him what had happened to each of the soldiers in the Forward Observer party up until we arrived at Manderfeld. Captain Smith complimented us on our daring escape and the fortitude we had in returning to the battery under such overwhelming odds.

Captain Smith quickly updated us on the events of the Battery since we left, but told us that our comrades would fill us in on the details. He then said he was short on officers and needed a Forward Observer. He told me that as a member of the Detail Section and my knowledge of fire direction he needed me to assume the duties of a Forward Observer. In actuality, I became an acting officer.

Although the guys in the Battery were extremely busy firing their howitzers around the clock and at close range, they took time out to welcome us back to the unit. They said they heard that we had been ambushed and thought we were dead or captured. They were truly amazed that we could escape and make it back through all the confusion of war.

One of the first things I did was to ask the supply Sergeant if my barracks bag was still around and it was. I then proceeded to put on three pair of clean dry socks. My feet were like ice as well as my hands. I should have reported to First Aid but I was fearful that they might keep me or send me to a field hospital for treatment and I might not get back to my battery. I should have gone because my feet became a problem for me in years to come.

Regardless, it was good to be back "home!"

Chapter 22

The Last Days With C/592

The war was not over by any means but just being back with my unit and my comrades was a real morale builder. And it was back to survival both as a unit and as an individual.

This day being December 21, 1944, meant that this was the sixth day of this fierce battle. Fortunately for me, my personal belongings and gear were still in one of the trucks and did not get lost or destroyed. I was able to get something to eat, shave and change my clothes but no chance to wash or bathe.

The 592nd FA Battalion was back in action, even though it was only in fair shape, and was in general support of both the 424th Infantry Regiment of the 106th and CCB, 9th Armored Division.

This same afternoon at about 3 p.m. an intensive German barrage opened up with "screaming meemies" and other artillery and mortars. The Germans were throwing everything but the kitchen sink. The barrage stopped about 5:30 p.m. at dark.

Word was rcccived that we must again move to a rearward position. About 10 p.m. that night we left Commanster for a new position. I was again functioning in my Scout Corporal capacity in addition to my duties as acting Battery Officer.

When we left for our new rearward position after the German barrage, it began to snow and the wind began to blow. We had a blinding snowstorm in full force. Because of the weather we did not arrive at our new position until about 3 a.m. on the morning of December 22nd.

The driving snow continued throughout the night and even into the next day. No one received any food, sleep or even any rest that night. I was very tired but used to this discomfort by now and I just figured that this is the way you fought a war. Shortly after daybreak we were again faced with "March order" to a new position to the rear because of the advance of the German Army. This maneuver is the most hated action to any

Army unit and one especially during daylight hours. No Army person ever wants to use the word "retreat."

The continuing snowstorm was a blessing in a way because the enemy could not detect our movements. It was the first occasion since our arrival in the Ardennes that the 106th Division had reason to bless the weather.

As I look back at that time and read various books, letters and articles about what took place during that battle it does seem ironic that the fortunes of war did play a role in our being caught up in this devastating mess where the 106th had to learn its first battle lesson the hard way.

In his book *St. Vith—Lion in the Way*, Colonel R. Ernest Dupuy wrote, "It was worse luck that the 106th Division occupied positions not of its own choosing. Those positions were in a rigid defense line that was originally laid out by the enemy for battle. The 106th's positions so far-flung, twenty-five miles in all, that only a skillful delaying action in depth, not a last-ditch defense in place, could have cushioned a coordinated enemy attack."

A soldier in battle thinks of self-survival but he also thinks of unit survival and that of his country as well. One cannot help but think, *Suppose we lose the war? What will happen to me, my family and my country*? Most soldiers do not want to be heroes; they just want to do their jobs.

When one considers what the 106th faced as a raw, fresh out of the states, ill-trained combat Division, it is truly a great showing of courage and dedication that even those that survived, in fact, did survive. For on December 16th, the first day of the Battle of the Bulge, it faced five German combat teams—the 116th Panzer, 18th and 62nd Volksgrenadier Divisions, Fuhrer Escort and 140th Panzer Brigades. Later the Division clashed also with the 1st and 2nd SS Panzer Divisions.

When I think back to those treacherous days where I waded through, not only the snow, but that entire German military might, it is truly a miracle that I ever made it. Many officers and men told me that when I finally returned to the American side. I am forever grateful to God for His divine guidance.

After going into position, on December 22nd, our Battalion continued to fire its howitzers in constant rhythm, almost unceasingly. Dog tired, no sleep, and food when you could get it. Our ammunition supplies had caught up with us so we could pour forth the barrages of firepower as called upon.

The 106th Division fought in snow and ice and rain and fog, fought in some instances without hope of relief, with just the dogged consciousness of snarling give-and-take, kill-or-be-killed. We fought with the enemy in front and rear and on the flanks an enemy who sometimes appeared treacherously clothed in our own uniforms. Now, for the moment, we were out of that hell as we pounded the enemy with all of our firepower throughout the entire day of December 23rd.

The next day was Sunday, December 24th, Christmas Eve. After the blinding snowstorm, which put down several inches of snow, the sky that morning was clear blue and the air was crisp and cold. This was the first time we had seen the sun for several weeks.

About mid-morning all eyes were raised to the sky. Bombers and fighter planes seemed to fill the sky. Here for the first time the weather permitted the Air Force to fly. Not without incident, for against the clear blue cloudless sky were multiple puffs of black smoke. The bombers were thousands of feet in the air, but not too high to escape the German Ack-Ack (anti-aircraft) guns. Also, the German Air Force was in pursuit of our fighter planes engaging them in dogfights. A Hollywood movie could never capture the true-to-life action we witnessed.

The greater flocks of American bombers, specks of silver shining in the air, were east bound to hit the German targets that the ground forces desperately needed, such as enemy positions, rail & supply, supply lines and depots. It was good to be alive that morning and it seemed that the good Lord wanted to help us.

What distracted us from the pleasure of watching the air assault was the numerous "hits" the German Ack-Ack fire made on our planes. Tumbling from the sky came some of the bombers and fighter planes. Black smoke pouring out of the silver shapes encased in red and yellow flames. It just seemed that the planes tumbled forever toward the ground.

One looks up in awe at a time like that, being thankful for your fellow comrades in the Air Corps for risking their lives as we were, but in a different way. As the burning planes began to fall, one just wondered about the airmen that were inside of those planes. Then the ever-present white parachutes began to float slowly to the ground. Thank God, some of them made it. However, I'm afraid some had to land in enemy territory or be killed as they floated helplessly to the ground.

Things were beginning to look up now, and we believed we had a good chance for survival. At least the Americans had stopped retreating. I hoped that we would soon be the aggressors.

The next day was Monday, but a special day because it was Christmas. However, the war went on like it was just another day. No Church services today. We fought instead. I had to wonder what everyone back home was doing. I took time out and wrote Mary Lou a few lines to tell her of what had happened to me without the details. I just wanted her to know that I was thinking of her and my folks and I was just glad to be alive.

To celebrate Christmas day, the 592nd continued to keep its howitzer hot, firing 481 rounds, which is considered a heavy concentration. At 5:30 p.m. we moved out again and this time went into position about 1500 yards northwest of Werbonmont. Here we got the approval to try to get warm. We chopped down trees and lit fires to bring warmth into our frozen bones. There is a limit to what flesh and blood can stand.

Also on Christmas day our Divisional Headquarters had totaled up the losses for the 106th Division. An unconfirmed tentative report showed that 415 were killed in action, 1,254 were wounded and 6,821 were missing in action. Of course many of the missing would eventually be counted as killed in action. The others were taken as Prisoners of War. This count out of the strength of 14,024 on December 15, 1944 meant that the Division suffered 60.5% casualties in just nine days.

The next day was a big day for the American forces. Reinforcement had arrived and now had the men and firepower to make an attack. At 9:15 a.m. the attack jumped off the slopes of

Hill 522 (designated coordinates commonly used by the military). The Infantry was supported by the firepower of the 591st FA. The 592nd FA also contributed a heavy wallop firing 340 rounds on the town of Manhay, which helped drive the Germans out of the village.

December 26th was the first time that the German Army had to fall back since their offensive began on December 16th. When we physically entered Manhay, we saw the destruction and the bodies of the German soldiers. Observers counted 350 Germans dead and eighty vehicles destroyed by the artillery fire.

From December 26th thorough December 30th we fired on enemy troop concentrations in the heavily wooded areas south of Manhay in addition to self-propelled guns and enemy artillery batteries. The 592nd continued on in support of XVIII Corps, as part of the 211th Group reinforcing the fires of the 82nd Airborne Division near Anthisnes. All of our action and that of the other American Divisions stopped the attack of the Germans 9th SS Panzer Division toward the north. During this period we fired 1,850 rounds of HE (High Explosive) shells.

On December 29th, we found ourselves in the vicinity of Anthisnes, Belgium, where the Division constituted XVIII Corps reserve, the battle-scarred survivors but only 5,534 strong. Reorganization and reequip was started. We would now exist as a Division but the authorized strength would be just 6,569 men. A far cry from the 14,024 we had just a couple of weeks before.

During all this firing, the mail Corporal found me helping at the guns and said that Captain Smith, the Battery Commander, wanted to see me. I finally found him at one of the other guns huddled over some maps. When I reported to him, he just looked up with his typical unsmiling face and said, "Corporal Roberts, effective immediately I am officially making you the Section Head of the Detail Section. You are now promoted to Staff Sergeant." He then smiled, shook hands with me and said, "Get back to work!" Just likc that.

I was truly elated with the promotion and my duties continued unchanged because I had been doing the work right along without the title. I was also still continuing in an acting officer capacity because we had yet to receive any replacements for the lost officers.

New Year's Eve arrived. If we were to plan to welcome in the New Year with fireworks, we did a masterful job because the howitzers were roaring at midnight and you could see the constant flashes of cannon and artillery fire all over the place and from both sides of the frontlines. This was our way of celebrating to welcome in the New Year—1945.

As of New Year's Day our Battalion fired 4,977 rounds of ammunition in 749 different missions, which certainly is no small contribution to the battle.

The 589th and 590th FA Battalions lost almost all of their equipment but we heard that they were able to destroy it before it fell into enemy hands. Divisional Artillery Headquarters, the 591st and 592nd lost only a few vehicles and a small amount of equipment. We were fortunate because our losses did not exceed 15% of the authorized allowances.

On January 2, 1945 we received additional artillerymen. The battered 589th, suffering more casualties than the 591st or the 592nd, divided up their survivors among the two Battalions and some went to the Infantry.

We again were having snowstorms. It was piled up everywhere. Every time we moved to a new position it took longer than usual because of the abominable condition of the snow-covered roads and in getting the guns into and out of the gun emplacements.

It was on January 16th that the counter attacking U.S. 1st and 3rd Armies finally linked up to close the bulge. It was one month to the day after the German Army opened the bulge in our defense lines. As the battle rages on we fired our howitzers around the clock and with great success. As a part of the forward observer group we destroyed many targets such as tanks, trucks, artillery, etc. On January 18th, we were ordered to move forward because the attack our Division and other Divisions made on January 13th began to push the Germans eastward in retreat. The Americans now had the manpower and equipment and were organized after the Bulge fiasco.

From this point on the American, British and French forces were very much in charge. We now had the Germans in retreat. We stopped their advance and destroyed much of their equipment, which was in short supply to start with. It should not be construed that the fighting was not intense at times or that no other Americans were lost in the battles that ensued. The Rhine River crossing and other such battles were not won without the cost of lives and equipment.

My involvement in the war in the next few months was doing my job and carrying on the responsibilities of the Section Head of the Detail Section. We began to receive officer replacements for those that were lost or killed. I then no longer functioned as an acting officer on a full time basis but only intermittently.

I can't recall when we finally received our first mail from home, but I do remember that several weeks had elapsed before the mail arrived. The one letter that I will never forget and one that I carried with me for many months wadded in my billfold was a V-Mail letter Mary Lou had written to me dated Friday, December 15, 1944 at 8:20 p.m. The reason this letter is so special is due to three parts within the letter. These excerpts are as follows:

> "This is my second letter to you today honey. I wrote you an 8 page letter at the office this afternoon..."
>
> "Just came home from church a few minutes ago...I prayed extra hard for you tonight sweetheart so that you may always be safe and that God may take good care of you..."
>
> "Mother goes to Mass every morning for you..."

Firstly, the fact that Mary Lou wrote her second letter that day was somewhat unique in itself. Why two letters in one day? Secondly, not the fact that she went to church that evening, but the fact that she prayed extra hard for me. Why would she pray extra hard that evening? Thirdly, there was the fact that her mother went to church every morning to pray for me.

The timing of her prayers was almost to the point of being uncanny! She must have had ESP that evening, or else she felt the hand of God himself. While she was writing the letter at 8:20 p.m. on December 15, 1944, it was already December 16, 1944 in Germany. Her letter was being written just one hour before the initial German artillery barrages that started the Battle of the Bulge, which resulted in my being ambushed and captured. I have always felt that God answered her prayers and saw me through the horrifying days ahead of me.

One day, about mid-January, our battery had advanced to a position near where we had lost one of our prime movers while retreating during the heat of the Bulge fighting. Lt. Sohier stated that he wanted to see if he could find it and see whether or not it had been destroyed or operable.

Lt. Sohier asked for volunteers to go with him. My two buddies, Bill Sewert and Carl Himberg, volunteered to go with Lt. Sohier. At the time the three of them were getting ready to leave Carl and Bill asked me to go along with them. At that particular time I just started to write a letter to Mary Lou. This was the first chance I had to write for sometime, so I just declined. They kidded me about writing to her and begged me to go with them. They said I could finish writing to her when I got back from our mission.

I actually began to put away my paper and pencil to go with them but a voice inside of me told me that I should stay where I was. I believe that the voice was the voice of God talking to me. Because had I gone with them, I may have been killed or wounded. We learned later in the day that German soldiers ambushed their Jeep and Carl Himberg was killed. In fact when they eventually found his body, it lay on the road and was riddled with bullets. Bill Sewert had part of his left hand shot up and Lt. Sohier was shot in the arm. Sewert and Lt. Sohier scrambled for a wooded area and escaped. Sewert did not return to our unit. He was returned to the States where he received a disability discharge. Lt. Sohier had his arm treated and came back to the battery with his arm in a sling. My decision not to go along was one more time I escaped being killed or wounded.

Had I not been so committed to my fiancée, perhaps my engagement to Mary Lou would have been very short.

I felt extremely bad about losing my two buddies, and especially that I would never see Himberg again. He was such a nice guy and he died too young, as did so many of the soldiers who served so gallantly in all the battles.

We began to get a little time for ourselves. I finally was able to take a bath. We set up a tent and the kitchen provided hot water. We took turns using the tent. We used our steel helmet to dip into a vat of boiling water, and then carried it into the tent where we took a "spit bath." Believe me, it felt really good. This was my first chance to change underwear in many weeks.

Throughout this time we continued to take our turns at guard duty, during the day and at night. When we had a chance to sleep we did so. Some positions we moved into gave us an opportunity to sleep in an abandoned barn or farmhouse. Most of the other times we slept on the ground in our bedrolls with our clothes on, mud and all. The best way I found to keep somewhat warm was to push snow into a pile and then dig out a trench in the snow. I then laid my bedroll inside the trench on top of the frozen ground. The blowing wind and snow would then sweep across the top of the bedroll. It was not unusual to wake up almost buried in snow.

The buzz bombs continued to fly; the Germans artillery continued their barrages and even an occasional German plane flew over to drop a bomb nearby.

It seemed like we were always on the move, forever changing positions. Many battles raged and many more American soldiers were lost. The Germans were desperate. They knew that they had to fight for their lives because the odds were against them now. Many stories can be told of heroism on the parts of individuals. Many books have been written and each story told is based on how each individual saw the war from his own viewpoint—me included.

Mail call was sporadic. Some days there was no mail, then on other days I received several letters. There were many letters that I never did receive because the people back home referred to things I never remembered reading in their previous letters. Mary Lou and Mom always sent me clippings from the Local Journal News, to keep me up to date on happenings back home.

The home front was doing much for the war effort. What the Japanese and the Germans did not realize was the fact that the United States could fight two wars at the same time on both sides of the world. In a very short time the industrial might of the United States was converted from peacetime production to war production. America had the will and the skill.

The harnessing of this industrial might was slow at first but eventually it poured forth over 296,000 airplanes, 86,333 tanks, 319,000 artillery pieces, 64,546 landing crafts, 11,900 warships and cargo vessels and 42 million bullets (1,400 for each enemy in uniform). The $100 billion economy became the $200 billion economy. Munitions plants alone employed 225,000 workers (more than half of them women) in 58 plants making shells, bombs and explosives–plants owned by the government and operated by companies which in peacetime produced roofing, Kodaks, Quaker Oats, Coca-cola, automobiles, etc.

The home front also continued with sacrifices. They felt the effects through rationing and other shortages of needed goods and services. In order to conserve on diminishing fuel supplies, a nationwide "dim out" was ordered. This meant that electricity in homes, stores and offices must be curtailed drastically. This dim out was not lifted until May, the day following the surrender of Germany.

The 592nd continued to move. On January 27th the 591st and 592nd moved to Am Kreuz and on February 3rd moved to Ambleve. Here we were attached to the 99th Infantry Division in its advance toward the Rhine River in Germany.

By this time of the year the snows had subsided and were replaced by rain. The usual February thaw had set in. Going into and out of position was extremely difficult because of the muck and mud, which kind of reminded me of the Division's maneuvers in Tennessee. Our boots and clothes were always muddy. It was still cold, but the bitter cold was not there, just the penetrating dampness.

On February 7th, the 592nd moved forward again. This time to Murrigen where we continued firing volleys on enemy troop concentrations and equipment targets. During all this time I continued to participate in the artillery control firing. I must admit, that it was a challenging game if you did not think of the loss of human lives being expended.

Due to our replacements arriving from the 589th and 590th FA, I now had practically a new Detail Section. My new guys were Oscar J. Plante (who spoke excellent French), Wilbert V. Ruona, M. L. Carmichael, Louis J. Krajnovich and Frank C. Colalella.

While in the service both Mary Lou and Mom sent me boxes of cookies periodically. I always looked forward to them. I never received all the boxes they sent but what I did receive were shared with others, as they shared their goodies also with the rest of the guys in our Section.

In appreciation, on one occasion my Section guys wrote Mary Lou a note expressing their gratitude, which I thought was very nice of them. They all signed their names and I forwarded their message to Mary Lou with one of my letters.

At the end of February, the 106th with its limited manpower lost an additional 126 men–18 killed, 87 wounded and 21 missing in action. And throughout the push by the American forces, they were taking German prisoners, which was a real switch from the earlier days.

Without going into detail, I must include mention of the fact that in many of the towns and villages in Belgium, we met local residents who were extremely pleased to see Americans. They were very friendly and many of them spoke English. Even with their limited supplies, they offered us Cognac, wine and bread. Of course, in our gratitude we'd give them cigarettes and candy. They were interesting to talk to. They all suffered greatly and many of them lost relatives and friends in the war. However, we were warned to be careful in fraternizing because many of them were German sympathizers who could even be spies.

Toward the wind down of the fierce fighting, every so often we had a Red Cross Club Mobile visit in the area of the gun emplacements where they offered coffee and donuts to the troops.

It was a pleasure to see a female from the United States and talk with them. In its own way, the Red Cross and its volunteer workers contributed to the morale of the fighting soldiers.

The Germans continued nightly and sometimes during the day with their "buzz bomb" attacks. At night when you are awakened by the eerie sound of the bomb, it can be frightening. You lie there and wait for the engine to shut off because you know the decent on the target is then evident. You just hope and pray that it doesn't fall on your position.

Even "Bed Check Charlie" never let up. The low flying German plane continued almost nightly, weather permitting, to harass the American soldiers, which was nerve wracking because you never knew whether he would drop a bomb.

By March 7, 1945, the American forces had regained ground and were now in positions that were occupied on December 16, 1944, the day of the German offensive that started the Battle of the Bulge. It took eighty-one days to regain our positions in that battleground, which only took a couple of weeks to move to rearward positions from the same area.

Also on March 7, 1945 the U.S. First Army crossed over the Rhine River at Remagen in Germany. This is the first time that any opposing force had penetrated that far into Germany during a war since the days of Napoleon.

On this date the 106th Infantry Division's combat role had ended. The 69th Infantry Division's move had pinched out the 106th in its drive for the Rhine. During its final week of battle the 106th lost 322 men. One man was killed, 320 were wounded and one was missing.

Throughout my days during the war I picked up various souvenirs. Some I sent home and some I later discarded. Others I eventually brought home with me. They have become mementos that probably mean nothing to anyone but me.

Chapter 23

589TH – A New Assignment

Early on the morning of March 14, 1945, the 106th Division left the battle zone and was withdrawn to St. Quentin, France for rest and reorganization. We left our field position and drove to St. Quentin a distance of about 315 kilometers (196 miles) arriving that evening. We were billeted in one section of the town that had been taken over by the Army. The houses abutted each other and were located on both sides of the street for several blocks. These homes would become our billets while we were there. The homes were located within the city limits near open areas because of the necessity that we have access to our parked vehicles, guns, etc.

While in St. Quentin, passes were issued enabling us to go into town if we so desired. This was a treat because a person really loses contact with the world when they are constantly in the field without too much news as to what is going on especially in the battle zone. We really didn't do too much while here, but we were aware that something was going to happen to our Division after we rested here for a few days.

St. Quentin was a picturesque town of fairly good size and was not ravished by the war. It was so different from what I had seen in the states. I went into town with my Section guys and Carmichael took his camera along. I was able to get a set of pictures of what I had seen in the town, which I in turn sent home to Mary Lou.

This was my first experience to see the canal barges transporting materials and using the manmade "locks." A small, steam locomotive ran on a track adjacent to the canal and pulled some of the barges. There were other barges that were being pulled by horse or oxen as they walked along side the canal levee.

One day the First Sergeant came to where I was billeted and said that Captain Smith wanted to see me. After reporting, he told me that the 106th Division had received approval to begin to reorganize since manpower replacements were arriving from other units as well as the States. Reorganization meant that the 589th and 590th Field Artillery Battalions and the 422nd and 423rd Infantry Regiments that were deactivated on January 2nd, after suffering such heavy losses during the Bulge would now be reactivated. It was rumored that the 106th would then return to battle in the South Pacific.

Effective April 1st, the Division was scheduled to move from St. Quentin to Rennes, France, an additional 436 kilometers (272 miles) west to begin the reorganization.

Captain Smith also said that the 589th and 590th artillerymen that were transferred to the 592nd at the time of its deactivation on January 2, 1945, would now be returned to their former units for reactivation and would act as cadre men. In addition, the units would need additional Cadre members who were experienced artillery non-commissioned officers to help train the new replacements in the Battalion's reorganization.

Now I finally found out why Captain Smith was telling me all this. He said that I was being transferred to Battery "A" of the 589th effective April 1st. He said that he did not want me to leave C-592, but the newly appointed Battery Commander of A-589 needed someone to head up the new Detail Section. When he said that First Lt. Ted Kiendl would be my new Battery Commander I was very elated. Lt. Kiendl happened to be one of my training instructors in basic training while at Ft. Jackson, SC in the summer of 1943.

He came to C-592 as a brand new "Shave Tail" (2nd Lt.) fresh out of OCS (Officers Training School) at Ft. Sill, OK. I had often wondered whether he survived the Bulge. He was a great guy and we got along extremely well.

Captain Smith said that it would be a good move for me and would offer a challenge. He then stated, "It just might work to your advantage." At the time the statement did not mean too much to me, but I would learn later what the remark meant.

Some of the 106th's troops would travel to Rennes in their unit vehicles, and others would go by rail. Those to go by rail would be the groups being reactivated who had not received their authorized allotment of vehicles, guns and other equipment. That would not happen until we reached Rennes. Just being transferred to A-589 put me into the category where I would travel to Rennes by rail.

Early on the morning of April 1st, I got up at the crack of dawn. I had mixed emotions about the new assignment. I was in a way looking forward to the challenge, but on the other hand I hated to leave the outfit that I joined when it was first activated

After breakfast, we were marched to our motor pool area where the trucks were waiting for us. We were then driven to a rail staging area, a railroad siding in St. Quentin, to board a train for Rennes, France.

What we found when we got to the railway siding was not passenger cars, but broken down French 40 X 8 freight (box) cars that had seen many better days. The cars were totally empty except for a large carton of "K" rations, which would be our meals while en route to Rennes over the next two days. We tossed our gear into our assigned boxcar and pulled ourselves into the double-door opening. As the ranking non-commissioned officer in our boxcar, I was placed in charge of the car during our ride across France. About 30 soldiers were assigned to each boxcar.

The engineer blew the train's whistle and within seconds the cars lurched forward and you could hear the chain reaction of the car couplings clear to the last car. As we began to pull away, from the noise of screeching wheels, I don't think the wheels had ever been greased. As we pulled onto the main line I could see that there were quite a few of these "troop" boxcars in our train and we were now on our way.

The weather that day was rather balmy. The sun was out and the air was fairly warm. At least it was not cold. If we wanted to see where we were going it was necessary to hold on to the edge of the boxcar door and lean out. It did not take long before we were up to full speed. In fact, with the speed of the train kicking up so much dirt from the railway bed and the soot blowing into the car from the engine's smoke stack, we found it necessary to close the doors almost all the way but just open far enough to let in some air and light. As the train stopped on a siding or whenever it slowed down we opened the doors all the way.

After getting underway occasionally our train stopped along a siding to let priority trains pass through. Other times we stopped momentarily on the main line for whatever reason. We used these opportunities for personal physical relief (piss call). Not at every stop, but periodically hot coffee was distributed.

If the stop we made were near a small town, many of the guys would scatter into town to try to find liquor to buy. No one in our boxcar missed the train when it pulled away from a stop. However, because no one knew how long the train would be halted, many times a few guys would have to run like crazy to catch the train as it pulled out and began to gain speed. Some of their buddies had to lean out and actually scoop the guys up and pull them inside the car. Some had to be scooped up by guys in some other car. In our car we had to pull in a couple of guys that belonged in other cars. At the next stop the "invaders" jumped out and returned to their assigned cars.

Trying to sleep in a noisy boxcar, bumping along, does not give you very much rest. However, we survived and arrived in Rennes on April 2nd. When we dismounted from the boxcars we were immediately loaded onto trucks lined up along the siding waiting for us. We were then driven to an area about five miles south of Rennes to an abandoned airfield that was built by the French when fighting the war with Germany.

After we reached our destination in the field, Lt. Kiendl came to look me up the next morning. When he found me we shook hands and he said "Roberts, its great to have you with me!" He then told me that he was short of officers and even though I would be in charge of the Detail Section as a S/Sgt, I would also function as an officer of Battery "A" until he could get a replacement. Our close relationship continued during the period of time that I was under his command.

In getting organized we were short of officers, as well as equipment, such as 105mm howitzers, trucks, etc. However, we began to receive the necessary equipment within the next couple of weeks.

To help us get our garrison set up as quickly as possible, we obtained German Prisoners of War (POWs) from a nearby compound at Rennes. Every morning several truck loads of POWs came to us and some of our guys took turns at guarding them. Our own troops did most of the actual construction but the menial tasks such as digging "slit trenches," sumps, carrying gravel for the roads and sidewalks were performed by the POWs. None of them were very enthusiastic about helping the Americans. Within a week we had a pretty decent looking camp, which included electricity in each tent.

One doesn't have to be in combat to get injured in the line of duty. One the guys in our battery, Don Humphrey, was running the electrical lines to the tents when someone turned on the power as he was splicing a line, which sent a jolt through his body that sent him to the hospital for two weeks. He survived, which was a miracle, to return to the battery with two badly scarred hands from the burns he received.

Our Battery received additional replacements from the states and for the next couple of weeks we were in to training full time. I quickly organized my Detail Section and began our fire control specialized training also. I had received my men for the Detail Section. My Section now consisted of John R. Schaffner, Logan Johnson, Art Mahon, M. L. Carmichael and Bob Courtney.

As a unit we went to a firing range where we fired bazookas, carbines, rifles and machine guns. I also fired my .45 caliber pistol on a pistol range. We also went on several motor marches. The only training we were missing was the opportunity to actually fire our howitzers on an artillery range.

While we were in training, on April 12th word was sent down that our Commander-in-Chief, President Franklin D. Roosevelt passed away at the age of 63.

President Roosevelt had gone to Warm Springs, Georgia for a short rest. On the morning of April 12th, he was busily signing documents while a painter was making sketches of him, when he suddenly slumped in his chair. He suffered from a cerebral hemorrhage and died very quickly. Vice President Harry S Truman was then sworn in as President.

On April 15th in a solemn ceremony, the 422nd and 423rd Infantry Regiments, the 589th and 590th Field Artillery Battalions and the 106th Reconnaissance Troop were reborn. Each unit received its respective colors, standards and guidons.

The war continued at the front while we were reorganizing. The Allied Armies had by now, swept across the Rhine River and had advanced more than 100 miles into Germany beyond the Rhine River. Some 198,000 German prisoners were already in Allied POW compounds. An additional 300,000 were encircled and trapped in the Ruhr valley. As Colonel Dupuy wrote in his book, "The fabric of armed Nazism was crumbling to dust."

We no more than celebrated our reorganization, when the 106th Division was split up. The units being reorganized, the 589th and 590th FA Battalions and the 422nd and 423rd Infantry Regiments remained in Rennes to continue training. The 424th Infantry, the 591st and 592nd FA Battalions (my former unit) moved to Mannheim, Germany to join another unit to take on an occupation assignment.

It seems ironic that the 106th Division should be selected to take custody of the entire bag of prisoners collected on the field of battle by the U.S. First, Third, Seventh and Ninth Armies, since the 106th lost more prisoners of war to the Germans than any other single Division in the European Theater of Operation (ETO). The 106th would eventually stand guard over 920,000 German soldiers.

In the final analysis, the 106th ended up processing more than 1,250,000 individuals of the "Master Race" of all ranks-from Field Marshall to Private; all ages from boys of seven to men of eighty-eight; and 2,600 women. I thank the good Lord once again that I was transferred to the 589th. We ended up with a more interesting couple of months than my old unit, the 592nd.

Not too far from our campsite was what appeared to be an abandoned castle. Before moving to the new location, some of us decided to do a little reconnoitering to see what we could find in the castle. John Schaffner came out of the castle wearing a silk top hat that he had found. It was so unusual to have something like a top hat in the combat zone that everyone took turns wearing the hat. Later Art Mahon came through the area wearing the topper while riding on the back of a donkey, which he rounded up in a nearby field. We sure had some good laughs at that sight. We laughed so hard that Carmichael forgot to take a picture of Art on the donkey.

Our segment of the split 106th Division was ordered back into active duty to the "Lorient Pocket" where we would support the 870th FA Battalion. The cities of Lorient and St. Nazaire, France are located along the coast of France on the Bay of Biscay. The Germans held both cities after being pushed back to the coast following the Allied invasion of France in June 1944. The "pocket" held by the Germans was approximately 100 square miles. The German soldiers fortified themselves with elaborate constructed bunkers that were impenetrable from artillery or small arms fire.

It could only be possible because of their permanent installations, but we found the bunkers to be the best camouflaged positions that we had ever seen, and probably the best that ever existed in any Army.

In the bay itself near each port city was a German U-Boat submarine base during the war. The submarines brought supplies in to the German garrison pocket. The submarine bases and the entire bay area was in turn, protected by elaborate mine fields in the sea, which the submarines could slide under when entering or leaving either base. The pocket was so well protected that the allies just surrounded it and left it be. The artillery and small arms firing on either side was more for harassment purposes than for anything else.

On May 6th, we our left Beignon in convoy arriving that evening at gun emplacement location. We only had to travel about 146 kilometers (88 miles). Upon arriving at the "Pocket" we immediately went into firing position. Then we learned that negotiations were under way between the Germans and Americans for the German surrender of the "pocket." The next day we received word that not only the Germans in the pocket surrendered, but also the unconditional surrender and the complete collapse of the entire German Army.

The first of our Battalion to go into the German pocket was Battery "C." We would follow shortly after them to help round up the German soldiers. It is hard to describe the gut feeling you get a time like that. It is one of elation, but also one of vengeance.

Upon entering the German occupied area, we found the gun emplacements, the bunkers and the area in general to be rather filthy. They resembled pigsties and reeked with odor.

Every available vehicle we could muster was used to load the prisoners and then transport them to the American POW camp at Rennes. As the trucks rolled through the small villages on the way to Rennes, the local townspeople were lined up along both sides of the road jeering at the German soldiers and throwing anything at them that they could get their hands on, including garbage. One of the guys in my Section, John Schaffner, was a guard riding "shot-gun" with the driver on one of the trucks carrying prisoners and he was showered with the debris also.

In our battery there was a mixture of celebration upon the news of the German surrender. Some guys were indeed happy and took it in stride while others got "stinking drunk." Some of us, who were overseas for a period of time, had accumulated a lot of "points" and looked forward to the possibility of going home. We were aware however, that an occupational force had to be established which would keep many of us overseas longer, but no one knew for how long.

In order to return to the United States to be discharged following the war, the Armed Services devised a point system, that would be fair to all, enlisted men and officers alike. Basically it called for a point to be allocated for each month of total military service, plus an extra point for overseas duty.

Participation in combat campaigns and battles warranted extra points as well as war injuries. Soldiers with 85 or more points would be selected first for discharge. The next group to be selected would be taken from the list in a declining number of points order. However, if your MOS (job description) was critical to that particular branch of service or the United States Government, then they had a right and a duty to keep you in the service longer. I would find out later that officers were automatically considered critical no matter what their MOS might be.

Shortly after VE-Day each soldier in the ETO was given a copy of a letter signed by General Dwight D. Eisenhower. I kept the letter for my memoirs because I thought it had a good message. Although the letter was rather lengthy, the final paragraph is the keynote part of the letter as far I am concerned. It stated:

> Every man, every woman of every nation here represented has served according to his or her ability, and the efforts of each have contributed to the outcome. This we shall remember—and in doing so we shall be revering each honored grave and be sending comfort to the loved ones of comrades who could not live to see this day.

After rounding up the Germans and placing the prisoners in the compounds at Rennes, we returned to our former camp that we had set up when we first arrived in April. Time began to get long on our hands, but we just sat there and waited for the next thing to happen to us. The weather was great so we just enjoyed ourselves.

On May 24th we finally left Rennes to rejoin the rest of the 106th Division in Germany. The trek across France and Belgium into Germany would be by convoy, a distance of about 912 kilometers (547 miles). What a long ride!

In my acting officer capacity I was able to ride in the front seat of the Jeep assigned to our section, along with the driver and a radio operator. My crew followed in a weapons carrier. Late in the afternoon of the first day we stopped near Neufchateau and bivouacked in the nearby woods.

The next morning was a big thrill. The MP's escorted our Battalion through Paris. Since Paris is so huge, I was only able to see the portions along our route, which consisted mainly of following the Seine River as it ambled through Paris.

At each bivouac point we either pitched our pup tents, or we just slept in our bed roll. Most of the time I just slept in my bedroll under the stars. The weather cooperated on this trip and I just enjoyed the tranquility of sleeping under the stars.

Our kitchen was with us and each morning and evening we had a hot meal. Lunch was either a “C” or “K” rations on the road. When you are pretty sure that you will not be shot at, then this kind of living is not all that bad!

This time the ride across France, Belgium and Germany was great. It was a far cry from the trek across France in December 1944 to the frontlines. The fighting was over, the weather in May was great and the scenery was superb, except for the destruction of homes, barns, bridges, cities, towns and villages.

For whatever reason, which I never fully understood, shortly after arriving at Nachtsheim, Germany, the Battalion received orders to take down all pyramidal tents except those being used for administrative and command purposes. We had to set up our pup tents once again.

Our mail caught up with us when we finally arrived at our destination at Nachtsheim on Sunday, May 27th after being on the road four days. I was back to writing Mary Lou every day and answering my other mail to Mom and Dad, neighbors and friends.

We were once again able to attend our respective religious services. The Catholic Chaplin set up an altar on the hood of his Jeep, which was common during the war, and those of us who were Catholic attended holy Mass services in a field nearby.

We were finally able to shower because a semi-truck fitted with portable showers rolled in to our area for our use. After we showered, the truck then moved on to another Battalion or Regiment’s location. We also began to get laundry service once again. Before, we were doing most of our own laundry with the hot water we were able to get from the kitchen.

Chapter 24

A Battlefield Commission

We only trained a half-day on Saturdays, the rest of the day and all day Sunday was free time. On a warm Saturday afternoon on June 9, 1945, I was lying in my pup tent taking a nap when the Battery Clerk pounded on my pup tent to wake me up. He said that he received a call from Battalion Headquarters and the message was for Sgt. Roberts to report "on the double" to Major Parker, the Commanding Officer of the 589th FA Battalion. The message was for me to have my Jeep driver bring me there immediately.

I was half groggy from just waking up and the message was kind of scary. The only thing I could think of was, "What did I do wrong?" I also wondered if Lt. Kiendl was aware of my sudden call to Headquarters. I hurriedly found my Jeep driver, Art Mahon, and told him where he had to take me. He asked me the same question in concern as what I was thinking myself.

The road to Battalion Headquarters was really a beat up path at the edge of the forest, which continued through an open field. When we arrived at the 589th Battalion Headquarters, I arrived in front of the pyramidal tent, the command headquarters of the 589th.

Behind a long beat-up table sat Major Arthur Parker. Major Parker commanded the 589th during the Battle of the Bulge. He and some of his men made a heroic stand against great odds in the defense of vital crossroads that became known as "Parker's Crossroads." Major Parker was seriously wounded in that battle. He recovered from his wounds and later returned to take full command of his Battalion when it was reorganized. Major Parker was not only a good soldier but also a good leader, who was highly respected by everyone.

Seated next to Major Parker were a Captain, a First Lt. and the Sergeant Major, whose names have escaped me. Coming out of the bright sun light into the semi-dark tent, I felt like I was about to go on trial and be court martialed. After saluting the officers at the table, I announced who I was and remained at attention. The Major then told me, "At Ease!" It was then that I noticed my Battery Commander, Lt. Kiendl standing off to one side in the darkened tent. Again, Lt. Kiendl had that ever-present big grin on his face. When I saw him and saw his grin, I knew that whatever was about to happen could not be all that bad.

Major Parker spoke up and said, "Upon the recommendation of your Battery Commander, effective today, you are appointed as a Second Lieutenant in the Army of the United States . . . Congratulations, Lieutenant Roberts." I was dumbfounded. The officers stood up to shake hands but Lt. Kiendl beat them to it. Then we all sat down and the aide to Major Parker read the Letter of Appointment to me.

HEADQUARTERS 589TH FIELD ARTILLERY BATTALION
APO #443, U. S. Army

1. Under the provisions of Circular 10, Headquarters European Theater of Operations, United States Army, 27 January 1945, it is recommended that the following individual, having clearly demonstrated his fitness for appointment by outstanding performance in actual combat, be appointed as second lieutenant Army of the United States.

John Marion Roberts, 35 791 572, Staff Sergeant

2. This individual has clearly demonstrated his fitness for appointment by outstanding performance in actual combat as follows: On morning of 16 December 1944, S/Sgt John M. Roberts, then assigned to C Battery, 592nd FA Bn was captured by the Germans. After escaping he made his way back to his organization and rejoined them at Vielsalm, Belgium on 21 December 1944. Meanwhile, all of the officers of his Battery, with the

exception of his Battery Commander, became casualties. S/Sgt Roberts was assigned the duty of Reconnaissance Officer. He continued to function in this capacity throughout the Ardennes campaign until the assignment of an additional officer on the 9th of January 1945. During this period, his Battalion, which was assigned to XVIII Airborne Corps, reinforcing the 82nd Airborne Division, was firing an average of 1400 rounds daily. S/Sgt Roberts took over the duties of a Forward Observer, and continued in that capacity until his battalion was withdrawn from the lines at Murrigen, Germany on about March 1. Throughout this time, S/Sgt Roberts had performed the duties of an officer with great credit to himself.

On April 1, S/Sgt Roberts was assigned to the 589th FA Battalion. Due to a shortage of officers, he was assigned the duties of Reconnaissance Officer. Throughout the Battalion's training period at Camp Coetquidan, France, he took full charge of the training and discipline of the Detail Section. On moving into combat in the Lorient sector on 6 May, S/Sgt Roberts continued his work as a Battery officer.

The leadership displayed in training was again displayed in combat, and S/Sgt Roberts demonstrated that he had the complete confidence of both officers and men in his Battery.

S/Sgt Roberts has continued in his assignment as Reconnaissance Officer until the present.

a. <u>Reconnaissance Officer (Duty Assignment) Battery A, 589th F A Bn (Unit)</u>
<u>1 April 1945 to date</u> (Period)

b. Campaigns in which the individual has previously engaged:
   1. Campaign Germany,
   2. Ardennes Campaign,
   3. Campaign Northern France

3. The 201 file of this individual does not contain any record of court martial proceedings having been instituted in his case, nor do records of this headquarters show any other reason why this individual should not be appointed in the Army of the United States.

ARTHUR C. PARKER III
Major, FA
Commanding

Afterwards, I was handed a copy of my Appointment letter and the telegram denoting my new ASN (Army Serial Number) as an officer (02006759). I was also given my discharge as an enlisted man, which is unique because the discharge paper shows that I was discharged in Nachtsheim, Germany.

Under the heading of "Decorations and Medals" during the period of time that I spent in the Army, my record shows the following: (1) Good Conduct Medal, (2) Sharp-Shooter Rifleman (30-caliber carbine), (3) Army of Occupation Medal - Germany, (4) EAME Campaign Medal with three Bronze Battle Stars and (5) World War II Victory Medal American Theatre.

The three campaigns I participated in during the war listed on my record were (1) Campaign of Germany, (2) Ardennes Campaign (Battle Of The Bulge) and (3) Northern France Campaign.

Following the reading of my appointment letter, Lt. Kiendl cut the S/Sgt stripes from the sleeves of my fatigue uniform and then pinned a gold, Second Lieutenants bar on the right side of my uniform collar and then a set of gold crossed cannons (artillery insignia) on the left side of my collar. I was thrilled to say the least, along with being quite nervous. I think I was calmer in combat than I was at this particular moment.

After returning to my battery site the guys were pleased for me. Their reaction was that they felt it was about time since I was doing much of the job anyway.

Later when Lt. Kiendl returned to the Battery, we had a long talk and he really made me feel welcome and important. All at once I remembered the statement that Captain Smith made to me when I left C-592 to transfer to A-589, "it just might work to your advantage," and it most certainly did! I always had a gut feeling that Captain Smith had a lot to do with my promotion as an officer.

Although the war in Europe was over, we trained as if we were going to be sent to the South Pacific. The rigid training, however, did seem to be superfluous since the Americans were winning the war against the Japanese, island by island. On June 21st, the Japanese surrendered yet another island—Okinawa. In order for the Americans to capture this island, American deaths ran to almost 13,000 and 40,000 were wounded.

Most of the guys felt that by now we would not be sent to the South Pacific as a unit. Even so, we needed to train the men because some individual soldiers just may end up in the South Pacific. It was also imperative to keep the troops busy at all times.

The Division was very liberal in issuing passes to anyone that wanted to go into Paris or the Riviera in France. In Belgium we could go in to Brussels, Eupen or Namur. Some even went to the United Kingdom. I chose to go to Namur for three days from June 29th to July 2nd. I found Namur to be interesting, enjoyable and very scenic. However, as I look back on it now, why I didn't choose the French Riviera, the United Kingdom or Paris, I don't really know! I now regret that I didn't go to one of the more glamorous places.

By now the number of troops per unit began to decrease because the "high point" men were being sent to one of the "embarkation camps" to be sent to the states for discharge.

On one of my visits to Headquarters where I had to see the Major Parker on some business, I had to wait outside his tent because the Major was busy. Seated in the waiting area of the command tent was a Lt. Colonel. We introduced ourselves and he told me that his name was Colonel Hagman who was one of the officers in our Division.

As the Colonel and I chatted for a few minutes, a 1st Lieutenant entered the area. The two of them greeted each other and then Col. Hagman asked me if I knew Lt. Tom Brown of the 106th Special Services Group. I had not, so we shook hands. Lt. Brown asked Colonel Hagman, "How's Mary?" The Colonel started to tell about his wife's latest stage adventure in New York City. I immediately became all ears.

As the conversation continued, I then found out that Colonel Hagman was talking about his wife, Mary Martin, who not only performed on stage but was a movie star as well.

They talked about the Hollywood scene where they dropped the names of stars like I would talk about my neighbors. I then recognized Tom Brown as a handsome movie star who played leading roles in Class "B" movies. Class "B" movies were usually feature films that ended up as a second feature in movie theaters. I recognized Tom Brown because when I worked at the Rialto Theater while in High School I had seen many of his movies.

After the war, I read in the newspaper that Colonel Hagman and Mary Martin got a divorce some time after he arrived home from the war. While they were married, they had a son together. This son was named Larry Hagman and would also become a famous movie star. In later years, Larry Hagman would play a leading role in the television series *Dallas* for many years.

Chapter 25

The Demise Of The 106th

On July 16th, we pulled out of our field position near Nachtsheim, Germany, and motor marched to an area in the vicinity of Mingolsheim, Germany, about twenty-five miles south of Mannheim. Training was a complete loss. It just became a matter of time before we would all be disbanded, one way or another.

While at this location, we had a new and unique experience to keep us busy. The Seventh Army solicited the help of the 589th to make a surprise inspection on one of the towns under its command. Plans for the inspection were held in the greatest of secrecy. Lt. Kiendl and his other Battery officers worked with our Battalion Headquarters and the Seventh Army personnel to coordinate the surprise. The 589th was assigned to the city of Kronau to make its inspection. Each Battery had an area to cover and we organized our search parties accordingly. At 4 a.m. on the morning of July 21st, we sprang into action. The town was surrounded with roadblocks so no one could leave until the inspection was completed.

The guys really enjoyed this assignment. We were to search everything in our area, including homes, stores, buildings of all kinds, and warehouses. A stern warning was given to be mindful and use extreme caution so as to avoid any booby traps that may have been planted. The early morning inspections in homes sure got a lot of people out of bed.

We were looking for firearms and other contraband, such as ammunition, radio transmitters, vehicles and other war materials. We also checked for black market operations being conducted. We had to check the ID papers of every civilian to make sure that each person had the proper credentials. This action was to reveal any German Army deserters who may be holed up with German families that continued to be sympathetic toward Nazism. Other displaced persons of other nationalities should also surface in such an inspection. Nothing of great significance was found through our search. To complete the inspection it took the Division about 48 hours. However, our sector assignment was completed by 8 p.m. that evening.

The manpower in the battery continued to be drained with the high point guys leaving for the states. Some new replacements were arriving but training had all but ceased at this point. The only question that remained was, "what happens now to the rest of us?" I found out on August 5th when I received my orders for transfer. I was reassigned from A-589th to C-589th. In C-Battery I became the Executive Officer.

The very next day the opportunity came for us to quit living out in the woods. I no more than reported to C-Battery when the Battalion got its orders to move again. This time the Battalion would split up. This was the beginning of the end of the 106th Infantry Division, but not for me personally. The split caused the batteries in the 589th to be billeted in different towns. My Battery-C was billeted in Woschbach, Germany, while the other batteries went to Karlsruhe, Kleinsteinbach, Stupferich and Berghausen.

August 6th was also the day that the American B-29 bomber, the Enola Gay, piloted by Col. Paul Tibbets, dropped the first Atomic bomb on Hiroshima, Japan.

I had no more than unpacked when I received word that the next day, August 7, 1945, I was being transferred along with eleven of my fellow 589th officers, for other duties. We were assigned to the 3rd Reinforcement Depot in Marburg, Germany. This transfer officially ended my Army career with the 106th Infantry Division, having served with it since its inception on March 15, 1943. The two years and five months I spent with the Division left me with both many great and sad memories. I almost got killed several times while serving with the Division and suffered many agonizing days, but I did survive. I had many experiences that I have never forgotten.

This time when we traveled by train, we were assigned to a rail passenger car. The cars were the old compartment type with wooden seats and each compartment's side doors opened onto a "running board" for stepping to the ground. Not fancy, but much better than a 40 x 8 boxcar. We arrived at Marburg after traveling a distance of 232 Kilometers (144 miles). While there, we were billeted in pyramidal tents with four officers in each tent.

The next day, August 10th, happened to be my 21st birthday. This was the third birthday that I would celebrate away from home. No one but me knew it was my birthday that day. I celebrated by going to the mess hall for all three meals and that was about it. I did meet a few guys there that I conversed with who were also passing through. The guys in my tent received their orders to move before I did. I just sat there and waited.

On August 14, 1945, I checked the bulletin board and saw that my name appeared on a set of travel orders, which ordered me the next day on August 15th to go to the Headquarters of the U.S. Seventh Army (212th Reinforcement Co.) in Heidelberg, Germany. I thought for sure that I was being assigned to the Army Headquarters for further duty. To my dismay, when I checked in that day to pick up my orders, I got an amusing awakening. The orders were for one day only to go by truck to Heidelberg to have my picture taken for identification purposes. Now I was convinced in my own mind that I was probably headed for the South Pacific for further duty.

It was well known that artillery Forward Observers were needed there. I certainly out-did my odds of living while in Europe and I did not want to play those same kinds of odds with the Japanese in the south Pacific.

The next morning when I woke up I heard loud talking and commotion going on. When I stepped outside the tent to find out what was going on, I then found out that the Japanese Army had surrendered unconditionally.

The news was broadcast by President Harry Truman in Washington at 7 p.m. EWT (Eastern War Time) on August 14th, which was 1 a.m. on August 15th (ETO) time. The *Stars And Stripes* newspaper issued a special edition with the headline, "PEACE." The formal signing of the Treaty would not take place until later, which turned out to be September 2, 1945. Portions of the article in *Stars And Stripes* stated:

> The greatest war in the history of mankind came to an end at 1 a.m. this morning (ETO time) when the United States, the Soviet Union, China and Great Britain officially announced that Japan had surrendered unconditionally.
>
> The end came after a flurry of diplomatic messages by Tokyo that it was ready to surrender.
>
> General Douglas MacArthur as Supreme Allied Commander will accept the surrender when arrangements are completed. Meanwhile, Allied armed forces were ordered to cease offensive action.

Obviously that announcement had a bearing on my future assignment. It was a time for celebration and I don't know where all the liquor came from, but the camp celebrated all day long. There were many hangovers the next day.

Several days later, my name appeared on the bulletin board to report to the personnel center at the Reinforcement Depot to pick up my travel orders. A Captain told me that I would travel to the Port of Antwerp, Belgium, for passage on one of the ships sailing to the United States. After arriving in the states I would be granted a thirty-day leave to spend any way I wanted to. While at home, I would receive further orders as to where I would report.

I thought that if I was able to get passage on one of the ships out of Antwerp then perhaps I might have an excellent chance of being discharged after arriving in the United States since the war in the south Pacific ended. I picked up my orders and the next morning a truck transported me, along with some other officers, to the train station at Marburg. We boarded a train for Antwerp, a distance of 355 kilometers (213 miles). I thought that since I was now an officer I might get better accommodations on a train. I was in for a rude awakening. Officers and enlisted men were treated the same.

We got off the trucks at a railroad siding and here facing

us was the familiar 40 x 8 boxcars. It was near noon on August 24th when the troop train pulled out of Marburg. The ride was almost a duplicate from what I experience when I rode the train from St. Quentin to Rennes in France. Same kind of stops, same "K" rations and same method of personal relief. At least this time I was going home.

Antwerp's Port of Embarkation was huge. It housed many ships of all sizes, from many different nations. From the dock area you could see the ships lined up in the distance waiting to enter the harbor area.

I would later learn that after I left the 106th Infantry Division, mass confusion set in. The drain of troops and the new replacements caused nothing but turmoil. Finally on September 1, 1945 the 106th Division, what was left of it, received the word that it was going home. The units were split up and each went their own way to the States on board whatever ship was available.

On October 2, 1945 the 106th Infantry Division was formally deactivated at Camp Shanks, NY. From March 15, 1943 the day the Division was activated at Ft. Jackson, SC until its deactivation on October l, 1945, three years, six months and sixteen days passed by. The Division died, but I did not, nor did my Army career.

At Antwerp I continued to wait it out just as I did in Marburg. Later we heard the news over the loud speaker that the Japanese had formally completed their unconditional surrender on September 2, 1945, which became the official V-J Day (Victory over Japan). The end of the war meant many different things to many different people. Husbands and sweethearts would be coming home. Others would mourn the loss of loved ones buried in a military grave in some foreign country. Soldiers would return home dismembered, disfigured and some crippled for life. And worst of all, to be forgotten in the years to come.

I remained here for sixteen more days and waited. The next time I saw my name appear was not on the chalkboard to sail, which I watched daily, but it appeared on the bulletin board for me to report to the personnel center to pick up my travel orders. I knew then that I was destined for further duty in Europe. On September 18th, I received my travel orders. The orders read as follows:

> Relieved from Shipment.
> Order No. 32, Page 27
> Assigned to 647 QM Trk Co.
> Salzburg, Austria
> Train #2
> 12:30 p.m.
> Arrival Date 20 September 1945

Chapter 26

On To Military Government

After receiving the word that I was being sent to Salzburg, Austria, I immediately wrote a letter to Mary Lou, and also to Mom and Dad. I wanted to tell them the news and that I had no idea where I would be stationed or when I could expect to go home.

I was disappointed because I was not going home, but with my new commission as a 2nd Lieutenant I was somewhat venturesome to see what kind of an officer's non-combatant assignment I would be getting with the Quartermaster Corps. I would sure see a lot of the scenery and it just might be enjoyable, except for the ice and snow during winter months. I also recognized that I could end up with a desk job of some kind.

On the morning of September 18, 1945, I gathered my gear and walked to the assembly area where many other officers were in the same situation as me. We all got caught in the deployment of troops headed for the South Pacific via the United States caper but were then ordered to remain in Europe. This is when I learned that all officers were placed on a critical list and were needed for occupational duty.

Knowing that I was quite a distance from Salzburg, I was delighted to find that I would board one of the trains containing several passenger cars. This was the same kind of car that I had experienced on one other occasion. Each car was divided into several individual compartments with a side door that opened onto a running board used as a step before reaching the ground. The distance from Antwerp, Belgium to Salzburg, Austria was about 811 kilometers (504 miles).

It would take our train two full days to get to Salzburg. The train was made up of many cars and the enlisted men and officers had to be dropped off at various cities and sidings along the way. Our route to Salzburg zigzagged throughout the trip as the old steam engine chugged through Belgium, The Netherlands and Germany before arriving in Austria.

For the most part I enjoyed the ride immensely. It was fun and exciting and the scenery and weather were perfect. We were served hot meals at breakfast and supper. At meal times the train pulled off on a siding twice daily but not always at normal meal times. It was necessary to carry our mess kits to the boxcars where the kitchen was located. The train did not remain at the siding very long at mealtime, so we had to hurry to eat and clean our mess kits before the train lunged forward on the next leg on our tour of Europe.

Lunch was the usual "C" or "K" rations as we rode along. Sleeping was done in the compartments by slouching in our seats and there was no way for us to shave, brush our teeth, or wash up. Some of the guys chose to drink, play cards, and shoot dice throughout the trip.

While traveling through Belgium and Germany headed for Austria, I would see the familiar famous slogan, "Kilroy Was Here" painted on the sides of rocks, barns, crippled German Army equipment, and bridges. The slogan was an imaginary abstract that was created by the GI's as they marched across Europe after landing in France on D-Day. In time of battle it was a morale builder for the GI's to see the markings and know that their buddies had been through the same territory before them.

We finally arrived at Salzburg, Austria in the afternoon on September 20th. Salzburg lies in the foothills of the mountains and is located just a few miles inside Austria across the border from Germany.

After dismounting from the train we were immediately taken by truck through the narrow cobblestone and brick streets of Salzburg to the place my orders directed me. I turned in my travel orders for further assignment to a Captain who was the Personnel Officer. (An Officer in the service has the responsibility of carrying his own travel orders.) After I gave him my orders, he glanced at them and then looked at me and, after a short conversation, blatantly stated, "You don't want to go to Supply… we desperately need officers in Military Government. How does that sound to you Lieutenant?" What did I know? I didn't have the foggiest notion as to where I was going anyways.

Without waiting for an answer from me, the Captain told me to sit there and wait for him. He was gone for about a half hour and when he came back he handed me a set of temporary orders transferring me to Military Government effective immediately and stating that the Quartermaster assignment was cancelled. He stated that permanent orders would be issued and that I will get a copy in due time.

I was then directed to a different building nearby. The Captain had already spoken to them about me and when I arrived, I was welcomed and greeted very warmly. I was told that I would be billeted in Badgestein for the night. The next day I would be sent to the Military Government detachment, I-5-A that was located in Kirchdorf, Austria for my permanent assignment as the Public Safety Officer. I didn't have the faintest idea what a Public Safety Officer did in Military Government and I was not about to ask. This assignment looked like it just might be a good deal for me.

In a very short time I found myself in the backseat of a 1938 Mercedes-Benz automobile. Two other officers joined me and we were then being driven to Badgestein for a night's lodging prior to our leaving there the next morning on the way to our new assignments.

Badgestein is located about 97 Kilometers (60 miles) south of Salzburg. It lies deep in the mountains of Austria and was untouched by the destruction of war. For many years Badgestein had been known as a plush resort town for the wealthy, so it was quite logical that the U.S. Government would take over hotels in the town and make them available as a place for officers and enlisted men to go on leave for rest and relaxation.

The hotel where I stayed was plush. Upon reporting to the desk clerk, I was assigned a room that had been reserved for me and I was told that the dining room would remain open until later that evening. I was also told that transportation to my new assignment would be available the next day around mid-morning.

I walked up the flight of stairs to the second floor of the hotel where my room was located. The tables, chairs, bed and nightstand were of the old Victorian era. The huge bed was canopied and the dresser almost touched the high ceiling. The long windows were adorned with full velvet drapes. I was overwhelmed with the plush grandeur.

I was amazed when I walked in the bathroom because here was something that I had never seen before in my life, except in the movies. The bathroom was tiled totally in white ceramic tiles with mosaic designs in selected tiles. The handles on the toilet, tub, etc. looked like gold. The washbasin was massive as well as the tub. The bathtub was sunken into the floor where it was necessary to first walk up a couple of steps before walking down inside the tub to reach the bottom. The lip of the huge square tub was even with the elevated floor. I began to fill the tub while I shaved and washed my hair as it took a while to fill that large tub with hot water. I then got into the tub and stretched out for a while to soak my entire body and relax. What a glorious spot to be in. I didn't care if I ever went to dinner that night. However, I finally did return to reality, where I donned a clean uniform and went to dinner. For a country boy barely twenty-one years of age, this was Heaven on Earth.

Following a bath and a good night's sleep and then a late breakfast, I reported to the desk at the Hotel for my transportation to Kirchdorf. Pfc. Ekis, who told me that he was from Detachment I-5-A, greeted me. He said that Lt. Bailey, Detachment Commander, had instructed him to meet me and drive me to Kirchdorf for my new assignment.

Upon arriving in Kirchdorf, I observed that it was a very small village with only a main street running through the center and a few side streets with a limited number of shops and stores. The I-5-A Detachment Headquarters was housed in a two-story building in the center of the village. A sign on the front of the building identified it accordingly. When I entered the building First Lt. Bailey, my new boss and the Commanding Officer, greeted me. After we chatted for a few minutes, Lt. Bailey gave me a tour of the Headquarters building.

Lt. Bailey told me that he had his own apartment and I would have my own apartment also. He asked Pfc. Ekis to take me there. After I unpacked I was to report back to him for my assignment. Now I would find out what a Public Safety Officer did in Military Government.

When I returned to the I-5-A Headquarters, Lt. Bailey told me that I would be the second in command of the Detachment. As the Public Safety Officer my job would be to "oversee" the village from an "operations" standpoint and his job was to "oversee" it from an "administrative" standpoint, even though the town had its own Bourgomeitser (Mayor) and other village officials.

The sector that we were assigned to was under the jurisdiction of the military of the United States. Our governing area comprised the entire Bezirk (county) of Kirchdorf. The local government officials continued to do their job but we had to be kept informed about everything going on in the Bezirk. We were on call twenty-four hours a day.

We kept in touch with the Mayor, the village department heads, including the Police Chief. We had to be on the lookout for contrabands, German sympathizers, black market operations and confiscation of property. In addition, we were to receive certain written reports, which had to accompany our reports and in turn be sent to our main Military Government Headquarters in Linz.

I enjoyed my assignment because it was a fun job. From an operations standpoint, I represented the "muscle power" in the town and I was always on the move. Wherever I went, the local people treated me as if I were a general.

Lt. Bailey and I each had an automobile assigned to us for both business and personal use. We both had a Mercedes-Benz. This was a plush assignment. Being small, the village had very little crime. The majority of the local residents were elated that the Americans had won the war since they disliked the German occupational force, so they made the Americans feel most welcome. Being fresh out of combat, I was always looking over my shoulder when I did my job because I learned that you never knew who could be trusted.

Shortly after arriving in Kirchdorf, it became necessary for me to change the shoulder patches on my uniforms. Army regulations stated that a soldier must wear the shoulder patch of his current assignment on his left shoulder. No rules indicate that a shoulder patch must be worn on the right shoulder, but it is acceptable for soldiers to wear the patch of their former unit on the right shoulder.

The new Civil Affairs of Austria emblem was shaped like a shield with a blue vertical sword crossed with a blue olive branch on a red and white background. This patch replaced the Golden Lion of the 106th Infantry Division, which would now be worn on my right shoulder. After obtaining the number of patches I needed, I had a local seamstress change the patches on all my uniforms.

While in Kirchdorf, I must admit I thought I died and went to heaven. After all, the war was over and the chances of getting killed or shot at were far less than when fighting in the war. In addition, I was living the life of an officer with its extra privileges.

As an officer I was entitled to receive certain monthly rations. The rations included five bottles of liquor and quite a few candy bars. Most of the liquor and candy I gave to the Lacheiner family, who owned the apartment where I was staying.

The village of Kirchdorf had a Catholic church where I was able to go to mass with the local townspeople each Sunday morning. There appeared to be many Catholic families in the area. Kirchdorf received no physical damage as a result of the war. The only physical element that did remind the townspeople that a war had taken place was the symbol in a field on the outskirts of town. Here, nestled in the grass, was a German bomber that had been shot down and glided to Kirchdorf where it landed on its belly. The pilot lived to tell of his experience. Surprisingly the plane was in fairly good shape and I had my picture taken standing along side the downed aircraft.

While in Kirchdorf my mother wrote me to tell me that Dad had to quit his job at Frechtling Dairy Co. because it was too strenuous for him and he could no longer keep up the pace. She stated that Dad would seek some other kind of work that he could do while waiting to collect Social Security in two years.

Many interesting things happened to me while I was in Kirchdorf but one of the more interesting evenings I spent in

Military Government happened shortly before I left Kirchdorf. Lt. Bailey and I were invited to attend a "Border Peace Party" that was being sponsored by the civilians along the border of both Austria and Bavaria. Local Austrian officials and guests along the border communities would be in attendance and it was to be a gala affair.

When Lt. Bailey and I arrived there for the pre-dinner festivities, we found the affair was being held in an abandoned warehouse. However, the place was immaculate and all kinds of streamers and banners, etc. were hanging from the rafters and the walls.

The hall was crowded with hundreds of people and most of them were Austrian and Bavarian civilians. In the group of military were a small group of British officers who were the current occupational forces in Bavaria.

There was a very large dance floor in front of the band and the "fraus" and the "frauleins" made the military men get out on the dance floor and do the polka and some of the other ethnic dances. I was really having a great time. The beer was flowing like water the whole time.

When dinnertime came we all sat down at long tables. After the many toasts of wine at the tables, a tradition in Austria during such an occasion was to pass a bottle of "peppermint schnapps" around the tables. Everyone had to pour themselves a shot from the bottle and toss it down the hatch. Each person used the same shot glass. Both women and men participated alike. Having never tried peppermint schnapps before I saw no problem in downing the drink like everyone else. Then the fun began and just what everyone was waiting for.

When my turn came to take a shot, I happened to be the first "foreigner" to get the bottle. A hush came over the crowd as I raised the shot glass and toasted the people. What I didn't realize was, the hush that came across the audience was in order for them to be able to hear and see my reaction when I downed the schnapps. I did just as the local folks did. I tossed the schnapps down my throat, according to tradition. The schnapps went down smooth. But, as soon as it hit the pit of my stomach, my throat, esophagus and stomach was on fire. I let out a yelp and grabbed for a glass of water. That gesture received a standing ovation of applause and laughter. It was a highlight that they liked to pull on foreigners and I reacted most appropriately and did exactly as was expected.

All good things must come to an end, because within the next several days and just before the end of October, Lt. Bailey told me that I was being transferred to the Military Government Headquarters in Linz.

LT. Bailey further explained that he had earlier received an inquiry from the Military Government Headquarters in Linz stating that they were building up their Headquarters staff and needed additional officers who were experienced and competent to work in the Property Control Section. He told me that he submitted my name with a recommendation that I be considered. He had just received a call that I had been selected for transfer to Linz effective November 1st.

So, after six short weeks and much to my regret, I was again on the move. It was necessary to say my goodbyes to my coworkers and the local townspeople that I befriended.

I immediately sent a Radiogram to Mary Lou to tell her of my new Military Government Civil Affairs mailing address in Linz as Detachment E-1A instead of I-5-A.

Chapter 27

Staff Assignment in Linz

On October 31, 1945, Pfc. Ekis, my driver from Kirchdorf drove me to the officer's billet at the Hotel Golden Kanone in Linz, Austria. Upon arrival I found that the hotel was small and intimate. This was to be my new home while in Linz.

The next morning, I reported for duty on my new assignment at the Military Government Civil Affairs Detachment E-1-A Headquarters not too far from the Hotel Kanone. The Detachment was under the command of Lt. Col. L. M. Hanna, with several administrative staff and section heads reporting directly to him.

Within the Headquarters there were individual sections and an officer holding the rank of either a Major or Captain headed each one. One of the sections was the Property Control Section. Each section was subdivided into departments. In Property Control there were two such departments: Real Estate and Business Enterprise.

Upon reporting for duty, I went to the office of Major Nathan Sirota, my new Commanding Officer who was in charge of the Property Control Section. During my first meeting with Major Sirota he told me that I would be the Officer-In-Charge of the Real Estate Department of Property Control. I knew nothing about being a Property Control Officer the same as not knowing anything about being a Public Safety Officer when I went to Kirchdorf, but I knew that I could learn.

I would find out later that at age 21 I was the youngest Department or Section head in the entire Military Government operations in Upper Austria, I carried the lowest rank as a 2nd Lieutenant and I had the least "time in grade" (five months). All the other officers were First Lieutenant or higher with many months in grade as an officer. I would hear comments later from several senior officers as to why I had such a responsible job with my limited time in grade as an officer and the fact that I was so young. I ignored the comments and continued to do my job.

The 83rd Infantry Division, nicknamed the Thunderbolt Division, was also stationed in Linz for occupational duty. They were the peacekeeping forces within the city. The 42nd Infantry Division, nicknamed the Rainbow Division, later replaced the 83rd. Both Divisions saw combat during the war, but like many combat divisions, the men in those units now were new arrivals from stateside to replace the war-weary soldiers that were sent home for discharge.

Linz, Austria is a fairly large city that is situated along the Danube River. It is located about 60 kilometers (48 miles) north of Kirchdorf and about 140 kilometers (84 miles) northeast of Salzburg in Ober-Osterrich (Upper Austria).

Linz suffered structural damage during the war years. The more heavy damage occurred when Allied bombers dropped their payloads on the "Herman Goering Steel Works" (formerly named Steyr Steel Works) located at the outskirts of the city. The bombings were effective because the steel mill was shut down completely.

The downtown area of Linz was quite typical of European towns. The principal downtown area was the town square with the familiar fountain and a monument (statue) on top. Around the perimeter of the square itself were shops and stores including an Army post exchange (PX) for the occupational forces. After Hitler annexed Austria to Germany in 1938, the Plaza (Square) was re-named Adolf Hitler Plaza. After all, Hitler was a native of Austria and spent some of his teenage years walking the streets of Linz.

Across the Danube River to the north lies Urfahr, that part of Austria that was occupied by the Russian Army following the war. The Russian soldiers were a continuous problem to the civilian population, as well as the American Government. Wherever the Russians occupied territory following the war, they stripped the occupied area of all its valuable possessions, including art, machinery, equipment, automobiles, and supplies, which were all sent back to Russia.

The reason I was so well acquainted with the Russian's behavior was because some of my civilian employees lived under Russian occupation in Urfahr and reported their experiences to me.

The Russian soldiers were very militant and ornery. For no apparent reason, the armed guards would periodically close off their side of the bridge and block people and vehicles from crossing in either direction. Sometimes the blockade lasted for several hours at a time.

The United States supported its occupation troops at its own expense, but Russia extracted both occupation costs and reparations from Austria. Russia's action caused Austria to rapidly become one of the poorest and hungriest countries in Europe following the war. Russia blocked every effort of the Allies to restore Austria's independence.

My first duty as Property Control Officer of Upper Austria was to very quickly acquaint myself with our purpose and mission. I also had to learn about the Austrian Civil Affairs that interlaced with my new position.

Although the Real Estate function was in operation before I arrived in Linz, it became my responsibility to build up the activity in order to expedite the operation. It was our responsibility to screen all Real Estate properties and place them under the control of the United States Military Government. Properties had to be classified in one of three categories: Nationals, Enemy or Allied.

I had to build a staff of field officers who needed to investigate property records in the "court house" and then travel throughout American occupied Upper Austria and place all such properties under Military Government control. The bottom line of our mission was to make sure that properties were eventually returned to their rightful and legal owners, which, in many cases, became very complicated.

Property records had to be searched in great detail at each courthouse in each hamlet of Upper Austria in order to determine the validity of ownership. The field officers had to be trained as to how this could be accomplished.

My office staff had the responsibility of issuing the official documents to all parties concerned to this effect, one of which was a notice printed on blue hard cardstock, which stated that the property was under the control of the U.S. Government.

One of my field officers would then travel to those properties and physically affix the notice to the front door of the property. My signature was the only authorized signature permitted on such notices. If the affected property was open land, then the notice had to be attached to a sign and planted on the property.

I would make many friends while on this assignment including my staff of eight field officers. My fellow department heads would become exceptionally good friends, such as Capt. Paul Truman, Lt. Lew Lehr, Lt. Bill Johnson, Lt. Chuck Seguin, Lt. Charles Duda, Lt. Bill Richey, Lt. Bob Miller, Lt. Tom Wetrich, Lt. Carl Murdock, Capt. Joe Levy and Capt. Charles Robertson.

Another person that I would become most friendly with was a fellow who was a few years older than me. We met at the Hotel Kanone where we both stayed. His name was Ernest Pretsfelder, a U.S. Government Counter Intelligence Agent stationed in Linz where he did undercover work.

Ernie (or Prets) was a good-looking fellow who spoke perfect German and, most of the time, he wore the native Austrian clothes including the traditional liederhosen (short leather pants with suspenders) and felt hat with the large feather plume. At his option he did wear a uniform of the U.S. Government, which was similar to that of an officer's uniform, but with different identification. Our paths crossed several times years later in civilian life.

One of the primary missions of the Military Government in Linz was to get the Civil Affairs of the country organized so that the management of the city and federal government could be returned to the Austrian civilian population as soon as possible.

A duty given to me shortly after I arrived was to see to it that I found an Austrian civilian who could eventually replace me whenever the U.S. Government relinquished its control. This individual who would eventually take over as my replacement had to be mature, well educated, and a native of Upper Austria who spoke English and did not sympathize with the German cause. Most of all, he had to be cleared by the CIC. Once chosen, this person would also act as my interpreter until my departure.

After several interviews and investigations, I was able to select a gentleman who met those qualifications. He had already been cleared and was currently employed by the Military Government and working in another department. His name was Dr. Rudolf "Count" Benigni. His ancestry and heritage gave him the legal right and title to be called "Count." He also had a Doctorate degree in business and languages from the University of Vienna.

A very important factor in making the selection was the fact that Dr. Benigni was a former member of the Austrian government before Hitler annexed Austria to Germany. Dr. Benigni was in his early fifties, was married, and had three children.

I had an excellent civilian office staff with no turnover except I did have a problem, however, in keeping a secretary. It seemed that as soon as I hired one from the Central Employment Office within the Landhaus, she was promoted and I would get another one. After following this pattern for several months, I contacted the Procurement Office and asked for someone who would be more stable.

The next time I was to interview secretaries, I was informed that someone capable of accepting more responsibilities than just being a secretary was being sent for an interview and perhaps show promise for a higher rating than just a secretary.

When the applicant arrived to be interviewed for the secretarial position, here standing in front of me was a tall handsome man in his mid-twenties who spoke excellent English. I learned that he graduated from Oxford University in England with a PhD degree in political science. Upon his return from England he was conscripted for military duty with the German Army.

Herr Schoeff, the applicant, who had just been released from an American Prisoner of War camp, was still wearing his German Army uniform when he applied for the job because he had no other clothes and no money. I hired him immediately. He was polite, intelligent and very efficient. Within a short time I promoted him to a better position and gave him additional responsibilities but also kept him as my secretary. I later learned that his parents had been killed in the war during an air raid.

At the Hotel Kanone, officers were billeted on the second floor and enlisted men were assigned to the third floor. Located on the first floor were two dining rooms (officers and enlisted men), a bar, game rooms, kitchen, and storage rooms.

Sleeping quarters at the Hotel Kanone were assigned according to rank. The nicer rooms were given to officers with the rank of Major or higher. They were also entitled to a private room. All other rooms required that two officers share a room without regard to rank. My roommate was Capt. Paul Truman, a former Infantry Company Commander who was from Plymouth, Indiana. We roomed together for several weeks until Paul fell hopelessly in love with a very attractive girl, Inge, who was a displaced person from Estonia. Paul moved out of the hotel to live with Inge and her mother.

After Paul moved out, I had many other roommates, none of which stayed very long. Some of the officers chose to rent an apartment or chalet rather than stay at the military billet. Then there were those who met a local fraulein and moved into her residence.

Shortly after arriving in Linz, I shopped at the Army Post Exchange (PX) where I bought several personal items, including Swiss made 7 x 50 binoculars for using on weekends in order to more fully enjoy the beautiful mountainous scenery. I also bought an Echo phone Commercial table radio with a short wave band to use in my hotel room. I could then listen to the local U.S. Army radio station where they gave out local news as well as news from the United States. The music they played was mostly American songs. A couple of the popular songs, were "Makin' Whoopee" and "Sentimental Journey".

After Dr. Benigni and I started working together I became quite impressed with him and he took an immediate liking to me. One day while at work he invited me to spend the weekend with him and his family at his country home in the mountains of Ternberg. Dr. Benigni made it clear that I was most welcome and he would not let me refuse the invitation. During the week while working in Linz, Dr. Benigni maintained a one-room apartment near the Landhause and only went home on the weekends.

I accepted Dr. Benigni's invitation for a weekend visit and accompanied him to his home one Friday evening after work in his personal car, which was an Austrian made Steyr automobile. After the initial visit, I went to his home on several weekends after that but always drove my own car (from the car pool), which gave me greater flexibility.

What I found when I first arrived at the Benignis' was not a house, but rather a large estate, named Rameishof. It was a very spacious, many-roomed, two-story home comprising many acres of ground in a valley in the mountains. The home was beautiful and well furnished with expensive inlaid wood furniture mostly of the Victorian era. The family heirlooms they showed me had to be quite valuable. I could tell that both Dr. and Mrs. Benigni came from money.

All members of the Benigni family spoke English. For the youngest child, it was a little more difficult to converse and some of the things I said had to be interpreted for her. Mrs. Benigni was a very charming lady and also well educated who at one time taught school. The Benigni's had three children, two girls and one boy, ranging in ages from ten to sixteen. They made me feel very welcome. Mrs. Benigni and the girls always prepared delicious meals.

My second floor bedroom was quite spacious and well furnished. I slept in a feather bed under down filled comforters. Each room had its own ceramic tiled fireplace. Whenever I had an occasion to go to my bedroom the room was always warm from the glowing embers in the fireplace, which a member of the family kept attending. At night the fire would die out while I was sleeping and I had to dress in a cold room in the morning.

On each visit I was treated like a king. After the evening dinner I would sit with the family by the fireplace and talk. I learned a lot about their personal lives and some of the local history of the Austrian people. I told them about my family and about life in America. Not only were the weekends with the Benignis' fun, but they were very educational as well. Following breakfast and weather permitting, some members of the family would take me for a walk into the mountains.

Whenever I went to the Benigni home I never went empty handed. I always purchased my full ration of goodies; these were the items that were almost impossible for civilians to purchase unless they bought them on the black market at outrageous prices. I took Count Benigni a carton of American cigarettes (the Europeans loved them) and a bottle of whiskey or cognac. Mrs. Benigni received a bottle of liqueur and candy. The children received candy bars and chewing gum.

Another of the many things I did while in Linz, was to become a ballroom dancer, and quite by accident. Lt. Wetrich asked me if I wanted to go to one of the local civilian hotels where a formal military ball was being held for all the American officers stationed in Linz. I had seen the notice on the bulletin board at the Landhaus but I had no interest in going.

Lt. Wetrich tried to talk me into getting a date but I told him that I was engaged to a girl back home and I emphatically refused to take a girl. He then suggested we just go without a date. He said we could get dressed in our dress uniforms and go to the dance just to see what was going on. I found that suggestion to be acceptable and it sounded like it might be fun.

We donned our dress uniforms on the night of the big dance and went to the hotel. We found the hotel's ballroom to be quite large, and many of the local frauleins were there as dance hostesses but quite a few of the officers brought their own dates. The dance seemed to be well organized, and punch (both regular and spiked) was available throughout the evening. A full orchestra played some American songs, but mostly Viennese waltzes. Lt. Wetrich and I just stood along the wall in the crowded ballroom sipping on the spiked punch and watching everyone dance.

Suddenly, one of the Austrian hostesses, a very attractive dark-haired girl dressed in a formal white gown walked up to me, and without saying a word, grabbed the glass out of my hand and placed in on a table. She then took my hand and pulled me out onto the dance floor. I had been watching her dance with some of the other officers earlier, so I knew that this young lady was an excellent dancer.

It was a good thing that my mother taught me how to

dance the waltz when I was in high school. This young woman did most of the leading, and as the tempo of the music picked up we began to dance in large swirling circles all around the full perimeter of the ballroom. The other dancers cleared the floor to give us room and to watch us. Now it was just the two of us on the dance floor. When the orchestra stopped playing, everyone applauded. The girl bowed to me as I thanked her. What a thrill for me!

I watched her after that as she picked other partners, but she never danced with any of the others the way she and I danced. That is the only time in my whole life that I felt like a professional ballroom dancer and this young lady did most of the work. I never learned the girl's name. In fact I have no idea if she could even speak English.

Christmas in 1945 was quite different than I experienced in combat in 1944 somewhere in Germany. A lot happened with my life during the past year and I was most pleased to be able to celebrate a peaceful Christmas in Linz. I would have much rather been spending it with Mary Lou and my family. I thought about them and wondered how they were celebrating the holidays. I went to mass on Christmas morning and at noon we had a turkey dinner with all the trimmings in the hotel dining room.

Major Sirota, the Section Head of Property Control, hosted a military and civilian Christmas dinner that year at the Landhaus (Real Estate & Business Enterprise). He hosted the dinner at a local restaurant and it was a very nice get together. Major Sirota was kind of a "stuffed shirt" but at this dinner he let his hair down. Maybe it was the wine!

I decided to have those in attendance sign the back of my menu so I could send it home to Mary Lou but unfortunately, not all the people there signed it.

The next day, I received a call at the office from Lt. Bailey, my former Detachment Commander in Kirchdorf. He said he was having a New Year's Eve party at the Headquarters and was inviting several of his officer friends. He said that I should not plan on returning back to Linz until the next day because he had sleeping arrangements made for everyone. And what a party Lt. Bailey hosted.

Each officer attending brought most of his monthly liquor ration. I never before, or since, drank so much booze and in such varieties. Lt. Bailey hired a bevy of local frauleins to cater the party. As the party progressed several of the officers began to seduce the girls and before long they paired off and disappeared. I admit getting quite inebriated by the wee hours of the morning and someone had to take me to a house so I could go to bed. When I woke up the next morning I had the worst headache and hangover I ever experienced. I vowed right then and there to never do that again.

Even though I kept extremely busy, I never faltered on writing Mary Lou or Mom and Dad. I also answered any letter that I received from relatives, friends and neighbors.

With the arrival of February, it brought with it a few mild days. Spring could not be too far away. I also had a few questions, such as, how much longer will I be here in Linz and when will I be able to go home? Since I did not have any answers, I decided to enjoy life and make the best of it. Right at this moment I could do nothing about it anyway.

Chapter 28

The Final Countdown

With the thoughts of springtime on its way I decided to see as much of Austria as I could. It is a beautiful country with so much to see. I utilized my time to good advantage by taking weekend trips to different parts of Austria. Most all of the towns I visited were located in the mountains and on a tarn (lake). Most of the towns in their heyday were resort areas and catered to tourists.

My stay in Austria and my assignment in Military Government were not all peaches and cream. I had a lot of headaches while in charge of the Real Estate Department.

As Real Estate Officer, my position called for me to meet with Austrian civilians from all walks of life. Meetings were commonplace with Austrian attorneys, diplomats, government representatives, etc. who were representing their individual or client interests. Some with whom I met did not speak English and Dr. Benigni was an excellent interpreter. I also greatly valued Dr. Benigni's advice and counsel, which I used quite frequently. I learned very early in life and especially on this job to use the wisdom and experience of others. No one single person can know everything.

I also had to be alert to the fact that some of the lawyers were exercising their cunning abilities as "con artists" by trying to take advantage of those persons who were displaced or of less fortunate circumstances. Some attorneys tried to get property returned to individuals that were not legally the rightful owners. I spent a lot of time with Capt. Joe Levy and his legal staff because many of the properties under control ended up in legal entanglements. Capt. Levy practiced law in Jersey City, NJ before joining the Army. I got to know him quite well.

I thoroughly enjoyed my weekends. I always tried to pal up with someone for a trip on a weekend. We would requisition a car from the motor pool and visit some of the little towns for the weekend. Sometimes we just went for a Sunday afternoon drive in which case the excursion resulted in having dinner at one of the town's local hotel restaurant's before returning to Linz.

The vehicles in the motor pool were military Jeeps and pre-war civilian cars varying from Mercedes-Benz luxury cars to other makes and models of lesser quality and prestige. One of the cars in the motor pool was an American made 1938 Chevrolet sedan. We also had the Austrian made Steyr automobiles. A fun car to drive was the Tatra automobile, made in Czechoslovakia. The Tatra had a sliding steel sunroof, a rear engine and a rear center fin similar to a rudder, which was a stabilizer for cornering. Whenever I went someplace with Lt. Johnson and Lt. Seguin we tried to sign out for the Tatra. It was an oil burner and whenever someone signed out for the car they were instructed to take several cans of oil with them.

I also ventured on trips with Ernie Pretsfelder. He usually dressed in his native Austrian dress and because of his excellent command of the German language it made getting around quite easy. He had quite a line for the "frauleins" as they sure went for his charm.

One of the officers I spent many weekends with was 1st Lt. Lew Lehr, who was assigned to the Legal Section in our Military Government Civil Affairs Detachment. When I did not go with Dr. Benigni to his estate in the mountains, I looked for other adventure. Lt. Lehr liked to roam the countryside as much as I did so we visited the beautiful resort villages and towns within driving distance of Linz. Lew and I got along exceptionally well and he was a fun guy to be with.

Occasionally I would wander alone on a Sunday drive. One such venture was when I decided to take a drive to Braunau am Inn, the birthplace of Adolf Hitler. When I signed the order taking a piece of property under control, my office staff told me that it was the very house that Hitler was born in. So out of curiosity, I wanted to see the property.

Braunau is a border town west of Linz and located on the border between Austria and Bavaria. Upon arriving in Braunau, I found a very small modest building along the side of a small dirt road. On the front door of the building was the notice signed by me taking Hitler's birthplace under control. He was born in that house on April 20, 1889. When Hitler was born there, the property was called the Gasthof zum Pommer.

Surely it was no claim to fame, but I always thought that it was kind of unique to see the control notice signed by me on the home of where Adolf Hitler was born. At least I thought it a bit different. One of the two photos I took shows the home on the side of the road and the other shows the front door of the building with the Control notice attached.

I received a letter from my mother stating that on April 12, 1946 my brother Bob was separated from active duty in the Navy at Great Lakes, Illinois as a Machinists Mate First Class (MM1/C). Bob elevated himself to the top rank as an enlisted man. The next step would have been a Chief Petty Officer. Rather than accept a full discharge from the Navy, Bob joined the Inactive Reserve to protect his rank. This decision would return him to the Navy in later years.

The hotel was really a nice place to stay. However, after living there for a while, I noticed that the quality of the food being served and the service was not what I thought it should be. In addition, many of the rules and regulations were being ignored or violated.

One of the hotel rule violations that really bothered many of the officers was the one stating that guests were not permitted above the first floor. It got so bad with officers and enlisted men taking women to their hotel rooms, that it looked like, as someone remarked, "a whore house at shift change." What really caused some of the officers to get irritated was the fact that at times they were locked out of their room because their roommate was shacked up with a girl. This situation happened to me on several occasions because my roommate was in the sack with someone. In addition, some military personnel were bribing the cooks and waitresses into delivering food up to their rooms during their "tête-à-tête."

At lunch and at dinner many of the officers were complaining about these undisciplined practices and rule violations but no one seemed to be doing anything about it. I also heard that food supplies were being stolen from the hotel storage room. I made up my mind that something should be done to bring these conditions to the attention of the Detachment Commanding Officer, Colonel L. M. Hanna. Colonel Hanna who was in his mid-thirties was a tough combat officer during the war.

I knew Colonel Hanna fairly well, because my buddy Lt. Johnson served in the same Infantry combat unit during the war and they became good friends in Military Government. Since Lt. Johnson and I were friends, I found myself in Colonel Hanna's company periodically. Since Colonel Hanna rented a chalet away from the hotel, he was not aware of the complaints. I thought he should be made aware of the problems and the morale of the officers under his command that were living at the Hotel Kanone.

The day that I went in to see Colonel Hanna was on May 9, 1946. Prior to my meeting with him I prepared a list of all the things I wanted to tell him that, in my judgment, were violations. As I rattled off the items on my list, Colonel Hanna was most courteous. He reared back in his swivel chair and listened to me very intently.

When I finished, he asked me how I thought corrections should be made. After I told him what I thought should be done, with a big grin on his face he said, "All right smart ass, effective immediately you are the Hotel Officer. Now fix it!" He called in his Adjutant and told him to issue orders announcing my appointment so that everyone would know that I was now in charge. Well, I was shocked with that announcement. He then added, "Of course, you will do this in addition to your other duties."

On May 16, 1946 a letter order was issued "By Order of Colonel Hanna" and distributed to "All Officers Detachment E-1-A" announcing that I was the Mess and Billeting Officer for the Golden Kanone Hotel, retroactive to May 6, 1946 the date I visited with Colonel Hanna. I now had the full responsibility of running the Hotel. This assignment caused me a lot of additional headaches and much extra work. I must say, I went to work and did the job the way I thought it should be done.

Knowing that I could not do the total job alone and the fact that enlisted men were billeted in the hotel as well as officers, I obtained the assistance of S/Sgt Sterling and Sgt.

Overby to help me turn things around. I gave them their instructions and the authority to oversee some of the critical areas of change. We had to release some of the civilians who were unqualified; issued new directives for the Austrian workers and re-issued rules to the officers and enlisted men billeted at the Hotel Kanone.

After a couple of weeks of hard work I could see that my efforts were paying off. I was really delighted. The theft of supplies stopped, the quality of food being served along with the service improved greatly. The general cleanliness and appearance rebounded. I ended up enjoying the task and gained a lot of experience from the assignment. Most of my colleagues were extremely grateful for my actions. Only a few were unhappy with what I was doing, but they were the main violators. I did receive a verbal commendation from Colonel Hanna.

Rank has a way of gaining respect from others, since it is a badge of authority. I can explain this with an incident I must relate that happened in the officer's dining room at the hotel. Even before I arrived at the Hotel Kanone, the military had engaged a four-piece orchestra that played music each day during the lunch and evening dinner periods. The orchestra could play many American songs and insisted upon playing requests from the officers while they were dining. One day they played a song that I never heard of before. After asking the name of it I found out it was titled "Jealousie." I frequently requested the song to be played while dining. It became my favorite.

Following my appointment as the Hotel Officer, whenever I walked into the main dining room and the orchestra saw me enter, they stopped playing whatever song they were playing, and immediately started to play "Jealousie." In fact it got to the point that whenever the guys heard the orchestra begin to play "Jealousie," and without seeing me walk in the dining room, they would say, "I guess Roberts just came in." I finally had to tell the orchestra that I appreciated their servitude but in the future, whenever I wanted to hear the song I would make a request like everyone else.

On May 15, 1946 I was promoted to First Lieutenant because of time in grade. I continued as an officer in the Field

Artillery branch of the Army. I would now wear silver bars on my uniform instead of gold bars.

I also started to pay more attention as to what was going on back in the United States. I knew that before very long I would have to face reality. I would be leaving the service and would have to find a decent job so that Mary Lou and I would be able to get married. Also, she and I would have to find a place to live.

One of the things to place a dark cloud on my future plans was the constant rumbling of the Cold War between the United States and Russia. The difference in ideologies between democracy and communism began to surmount. The poverty that was taking over Europe was appalling and the liberated countries were looking to the United States for aid. The American people began to fear that another war was inevitable. Only this time it would be with Russia, because of the tension mounting between the two super powers. My own staff was willing to make a bet with me that war between the United States and Russia would happen within the next two years.

From what I read and what I saw, I began to believe that war was quite possible between Russia and the United States. I also began to wonder if I would even get out of Europe because the U.S. Government just might put a freeze on returning troops to the states for discharge

In May I received a startling telephone message from the 6824 Civil Affairs Headquarters. I was told that I should contact my mother immediately. Obviously this message came as a shock to me. I knew that something terrible must have happened at home. I immediately sent a Radiogram to my mother stating I received such a message and asked her for a cable answer.

I received a Radiogram answer from Mom on May 25, 1946 that stated, "Everything O.K. Letter will follow." Mom's follow-up letter advised me that Dad had suffered a heart attack but he was on medication and recovering nicely and for me not to worry. I knew that my brother Bob was home from the Navy and could now help take care of our parents.

In spite of the rumors and everything else, I did have a gut feeling that my days in Europe were winding down. I continued to take advantage of every opportunity to do something different such as taking a couple of boat cruises on the Danube River toward the end of May.

The following weekend, my buddy Lt. Johnson invited mc on a private river launch cruise on the Danube. He said that Colonel Hanna hired a private launch for a Sunday boat ride down the Danube and Colonel Hanna told Johnson that he was allowed to invite a couple of other officers with their dates. He invited Lt. Seguin and me. Johnson was aware that I didn't date but knew I would enjoy the boat ride.

We left on a very cloudy and cool Sunday afternoon from a private boat dock in Linz. However, the motor launch was very comfortable. Colonel Hanna had a date, as did Lt. Johnson and Lt. Seguin. I really enjoyed that private ride along the banks of the Danube. I learned that Colonel Hanna had made dinner reservations for the group before returning to Linz that evening. The restaurant was elevated on a hillside near a small private boat dock. The scenic view of the valley and the Danube River from the dining room was spectacular. It was a very enjoyable day to remember.

In early June, I received word from Major Sirota that he was able to get my release. Major Sirota was very complementary about the kind of job I did for him and wished me a safe trip home and much success in civilian life. My position would now be turned over to Dr. Benigni.

I then learned that several of the other guys in Military Government would also be leaving for the states with me. To be able to travel with someone I knew would make for a great trip home. My travel orders dictated that I was to return to New York City. From there I would be transported to one of the nearby camps for processing and discharge. My orders stated that I was scheduled to sail from Le Harve, France on June 30, 1946. This meant that I would get another train ride across Europe, but what a train ride this one would be. Going home at last. I had not seen Mary Lou or Mom, Dad and my brother Bob for about two years.

With this exciting news, I immediately sent two telegrams, one to Mom and Dad and one to Mary Lou. The one to Mary Lou had the following message:

LEAVING LINZ FOR HOME MONDAY 17TH
HAPPY DAY
LOVE AND KISSES =
JACK.

My military travels in the past three and one-half years took me through many parts of the United States, across the Atlantic Ocean to England and then across the English Channel. My excursions in Europe took me across the land several times in many different countries under all kinds of circumstances and weather conditions.

I thanked God for seeing me through the many disasters I faced. I also thanked God for the many good times that I had and the many experiences that I would remember for a long time. I was glad just to be alive. I traveled thousands of miles during this time, but no miles would be so great as the final miles I would travel home.

Sometime after I arrived home, I learned that shortly after assuming my responsibilities, Dr. Benigni resigned his position with the Military Government to assume a leadership role with the Austrian government. Herr Schoeff, my former secretary, in turn, replaced him. I learned this information because I corresponded briefly with Dr. Benigni.

After spending almost eight months in Linz, I got to know a lot of people and make many friends, both civilian and military. I knew I would miss them, as they were an important segment of my life and a big part of the time I spent as a commissioned officer.

I said Goodbye to my friends. You know who your friends are when you leave them. I had many. I will skip the details of such partings, but I must admit that they were emotional.

Chapter 29

U.S.A., Here I Come!

Monday morning June 17th arrived. I did not need an alarm clock to get me up this morning. After having a restless night I got up rather early and bathed. I knew this would be the last time I would bathe for several days because our trip across Europe to Le Harve, France would be about 2,000 kilometers (1,200 miles), a long and hot train ride.

I went to breakfast in the dining room at the hotel. I think I was the first one to arrive there that morning. After breakfast a truck was scheduled to pick me up, along with some other guys, for transportation to Salzburg where we would get on a train for our long journey across Europe. My scheduled date for boarding a ship was June 30th.

After breakfast I returned to my room to pick up my Val pack (valise). My personal locker had already been shipped home. Talk about someone who was full of anticipation, I was bubbling all over with excitement, as were some of the other guys. To think that I was finally going home to be discharged after being away from home for thirty-nine months and being overseas for twenty months.

Gathering on the sidewalk in front of the Hotel Kanone waiting for our transportation were several officers, including several of my friends.... Lt. Lehr, Lt. Miller, Capt. Robertson and Capt. Truman. When our scheduled truck arrived, we tossed our Val packs over the tailgate of the truck. Some of my Army buddies and several of the employees at the Hotel Kanone were there to shake hands with me before boarding the truck.

Our group leader, a Major, who was also leaving with us for the ride to Salzburg called out, "mount up," and we crawled in over thc tailgate of the 2 ½ ton GMC truck. As the truck pulled away I waved farewell to my friends.

As the truck rumbled and bounced along on the way to Salzburg, we joked, laughed and were generally ecstatic about the thought of going home. There were a couple of guys, however, who had mixed emotions about returning to the States because they were leaving a girlfriend in Linz. One of my friends, Capt. Paul Truman was one of those guys. Paul's romance with Inge would enter my life within the next year. Inge later asked me to give her away in marriage to Paul and I gladly accepted the honor.

The ride to Salzburg was a short one. Being summertime, at least the weather was warm. We arrived at the railroad station in Salzburg where a train, consisting of several cars, was waiting for us to board.

This time our train departure was much better organized than previous experiences. I was immediately assigned to one of the rail passenger cars that had separate compartments where several officers would sit together. Lt. Lew Lehr was one of my compartment officers.

Throughout our ride to Le Harve I saw, at different times, trains loaded with displaced persons. At one of the railroad sidings where we stopped once, sitting on a track near our train was one of these trains. Here we witnessed a full trainload of cars that were loaded with displaced persons being returned to their homeland. These displaced people were being transported in open "coal" cars where it was necessary for them to stand up. They had no protection from the elements. It was a sight that I would ever forget.

These poor people were being herded and transported like cattle. For the most part, they were shabbily dressed and I understand that all of their earthly possessions were carried with them. Their ages ranged from the very young to the very old. Not one of these people were smiling. Their facial expressions told the whole story. One picture was worth a thousand words. At least they were survivors of the gruesome war.

After two days on the rails, on Thursday, June 20th we finally arrived at one of the Army embarkation camps located near the port of Le Harve, France. Trucks were waiting when we arrived at the railroad siding. As we dismounted, we were immediately loaded onto trucks and taken to an area nearby where we were assigned to one of the many tents. I would share this tent with seven other officers. Among my tent mates were

Lt. Lehr, Lt. Miller, Capt. Truman and Lt. Brochier.

My sailing date was Sunday, June 30th. I knew that I only had to wait ten days before departure. To pass the time, I picked up a couple of books to read from one of the nearby day rooms. I also played cards with the guys in my tent and walked around the area. In the evenings several of the officers walked to the PX where we could get a beer. The weather in France was quite warm during July, so during the day time hours some of us moved our cots outside the tent and absorbed some of the sunshine. Lehr, Miller, Truman and I were four of the "sunshine boys."

On Sunday, June 30th my sailing date finally arrived. Our loading time was scheduled for after lunch. Since this day was a Sunday, I went to the local Chapel to attend mass right after breakfast and then finished what little packing I had to do.

At about 2 p.m., those of us who were scheduled to board the SS LEHIGH VICTORY received our notice to report to the main assembly area nearby. I pulled myself up over the tailgate of a GMC 2 ½ ton truck and then stuck out my hand to help pull my traveling buddies in the truck. These were my tent buddies and we all pretty much stayed together for the past ten days.

The ride to port side was not very far. We alit from the truck and there facing us was the SS LEHIGH VICTORY. I grabbed my Val pack and with a big grin on my face I walked up the gangplank. This time the transfer of troops was well organized. Each soldier was directed to his assigned compartment.

Included in our total passenger count were twelve women on board. Ten of them were officers who served as nurses or in some administrative capacity while overseas. The other two were U.S. civilians, one from the Censorship Corps and the other from the American Red Cross.

The Officers Quarters on this Victory ship were no different than the enlisted men's quarters. The Army just kept the two groups separated because of rank. Being one of the first to board ship, I was able to grab a bunk that was nearer to the steel deck. Since this ship was much smaller and lighter than the USCGSS WAKEFIELD, I figured if we ran into the same kind of storm conditions as I experienced on the way to Europe and the ship starts rocking and rolling on such high waves, I won't have far to fall before hitting the deck, should I get thrown out.

I left chow in the galley and went topside to look around. I stayed on deck until we shoved off which happened at 8:42 p.m. on June 30th. As we were slowly pulling away from the dock area with the help of a couple of tugboats, chills ran up and down my spine.

I spent as much time as I could on deck. I began to reminisce about all the things that happened to me since I arrived overseas. Some experiences were fearful and some quite eventful. I thanked the good Lord for seeing me through it all and I knew that I was a better person for having faced such experiences. I also asked Him for a safe trip home across the 3,309 miles it would take us to cross the Atlantic before arriving in the United States.

I continued to watch the lights on the distant shore as darkness began to fall. I continued to watch the flickering lights until they were finally swallowed up in pitch-blackness. I left the deck area and descended the ladder to my compartment. My body needed a good rest.

There was not a whole lot to do or see on an LST troop ship. Since I no longer had letters to write, I did other things to make up for that extra time. I roamed the entire ship many times. The wartime guns were still mounted on the various decks but they were covered over with a tarpaulin. I spent a lot of time on deck just watching the ocean roll on and on.

I was again fascinated with the fact that I was sailing the Atlantic Ocean. I truly enjoyed the thrilling experience. At least on this trip I was headed home to a new life filled with much hope and not heading for a strange continent at war and into the unknown. Also, on this trip, I knew a lurking German U-boat would not sink us and that was a welcome relief.

Even though it was against the rules, the main pass time for the troops, including officers, was gambling in the compartments. No one made any attempt to stop the gambling either. There were many poker games and dice games going on night and day. I never got into the gambling. A dollar meant too much to me. The stakes were quite high and there were fortunes won and lost during the time we were at sea. It was a well-known fact that when our ship docked in New York, some guys got off with a barracks bag full of paper money.

The second day at sea was the first day that we received any communication aboard ship. With the help of some volunteers aboard ship, they put together a two-page mimeographed newsletter called *The Lehigh Victory News* and distributed copies to the various compartments.

The newsletter gave us information about some of the happenings aboard ship as well an update on what was happening around the world which the staff had picked up from the short wave radio in the radio room aboard ship.

Thursday was July 4th, Independence Day. There was nothing special to this day and there were no celebrations on board ship. The only thing we were concerned about was the number of miles we traveled and the number of miles we still had to go. By noon this day we traveled another leg of our journey in the past 24-hours covering an additional 386 miles. Only 1,953 miles to go!

Saturday, July 6th was my brother Bob's 24th birthday. I never missed wishing any of my family members a Happy Birthday while I was in service. I may have been late, because of the circumstances or the lateness of mail delivery, but I never forgot. However, on board ship I had to let Bob's birthday pass by without the usual greeting.

Throughout our trip, each time we crossed a time zone it was announced over the loud speakers so we could set out watches back accordingly. The news update was a far cry from when I went overseas. We were told nothing.

Tuesday, July 9th—The final leg of our ocean voyage. After breakfast the number of guys going on deck to see the United States come into view over the bow of the ship was amazing. Not all the guys went topside, there were those that continued their games of chance, hoping to win that fortune before the ship docked.

Looming over the bow of the SS LEHIGH VICTORY we could see the smooth horizon in the distance. Shortly, we could see a few bumps on the horizon. We knew that this had to be New York—the United States of America. You never heard such howling in your life. "We made it!"

As we neared New York City and entered the Lower Bay between Brooklyn and Staten Island, we could see the Statue of Liberty with her arm extended welcoming her sons' home from the war. As our ship sailed by the statue, I must admit that chills ran down my spine and caused a lump to swell up in my throat. This is America! This is home!

As Captain Jones, our ship's captain, had announced, we were right on schedule. It was about 11 a.m. when we entered the New York harbor area at Staten Island. At this point we were now under the control of the tugboats guiding us into our assigned port.

My what a good feeling. It is impossible to explain the kind of emotions one feels at a time like this. All kinds of thoughts are rushing through one's mind. There is a matter of being proud also. Proud that you served your country with the capabilities you had to offer. I was especially proud because when I departed the United States some twenty-one months before, I left with a rank of Corporal and had elevated myself to that of a First Lieutenant and was only twenty-one years of age.

As we edged into our assigned slip, I was standing by the rail of the ship and there were several rows of guys behind me. Since I got on deck early, I had a front row view. By now I think most of the guys were out of the hull of the ship. A band was playing on the dock to greet our arrival and a couple of girl vocalists were singing the popular songs of that era.

To my surprise, there were quite a few civilians at the harbor waiting for our ship to dock. Some were just sightseers, but some were family members of men on board. Some of the guys, after learning what ship they were sailing on and when our ship was leaving, sent a cable home before leaving Le Harve. Their family members were then able to find out when and where the SS LEHIGH VICTORY would dock. The waving and hollering was fantastic and it made more chills run up and down my spine.

When I stepped off the gangplank and firmly placed my

foot on the dock, I knew that I was once again on American soil, even though it was a wooden dock attached to steel pillars.

It was heart warming to see some of the guys rush to the throng of civilians to single out his wife, mother or girlfriend and sweep them off their feet. At the same time giving them a big hug and kiss. I wondered about my welcome home in just a few days.

It was hot in New York when we got off the ship. After assembling in small groups, we were then directed to another area for immediate transportation by truck to Camp Kilmer, NJ for further processing toward our eventual separation.

Chapter 30

The Separation Process

I was fortunate that I was able to remain with three guys that I knew fairly well. It extended the camaraderie into the separation process. We rode on the same truck to Camp Kilmer. Although Camp Kilmer was in New Jersey, it was only about fifteen miles from Staten Island and just across the Hudson River and right outside of New York City itself. The three guys were Capt., Truman, Lt. Lehr, and Lt. Miller.

Upon arriving at Camp Kilmer we were billeted in the typical wooden barracks containing cots and steel wall lockers. We were informed that the next day Wednesday, July 10th, we would start our processing for separation, which included our final Army physical. The evening was ours to do as we pleased.

The first thing the four of us agreed upon was to call Captain Joe Levy who had been our Legal Officer in Military Government in Linz and was currently an attorney in private practice. Capt. Levy told some of us when he departed from Linz that whenever we arrived in the states we should call him.

Joe lived in Jersey City, NJ and not too far from Camp Kilmer. He was glad that we called and he told us that he would come to camp to pick us up and take us out to dinner. This sounded great since we had not eaten anything since breakfast that morning.

The next thing I did was called Mom and Dad to tell them that I had arrived safely in the United States. Knowing that Mary Lou was at work, I could not call her, so I asked Mom to let her know that I had arrived and I would call her later. She was sure glad to hear my voice.

By the time we took our long overdue hot shower with non-salt water and changed into our dress uniforms, Joe Levy had arrived at our barracks in his automobile. After the glad tidings on seeing each other, we piled in his car and departed for his home, arriving there about 5 p.m. Joe lived in a large two-story house with his sister and brother-in-law.

Upon arrival at Joe's house, he introduced us to his sister and her husband. Joe fixed us a drink and said that he made plans for us that evening. He said that he was going to take us into New York City for dinner and then to see the sights and the bright lights. I had never been to New York, so this sounded exciting to me.

The restaurant where he took us was very plush. For a country boy, I had never seen anything so fancy in my life. We all ordered a steak and it was here that I was encouraged to order a shrimp cocktail. I had never eaten shrimp before and it sure tasted good. We also had a cocktail before dinner and then dessert afterwards. Joe picked up the tab for the whole meal even though we tried to pay our portion.

We then hailed a cab and went to Greenwich Village. We entered a nightclub named the Carnival. The entertainment that evening was a young comic by the name of Milton Berle. I never laughed so hard in my life. He put on a great show. Back then he was a little raunchy, but he had natural comedic talent. From then on, I was one of his greatest fans.

We then went to Times Square and walked the streets for a while. For late on a Tuesday night the streets were really crowded with people. Joe said it was like that every night and more so on the weekends. We looked at the tall buildings, into the store windows and watched the people. Times Square was quite a sight and I will never forget the magnitude of the street, people and buildings. I was enthralled. Walking the city streets in those days, a person felt completely safe.

We then went to a smoke-filled, offbeat nightclub, which was rather small. It had a small orchestra with a female vocalist and featured a couple of very raunchy comedians telling dirty jokes with appropriate gestures.

The emcee stopped the music for an audience participation game that was to be played in front of the bandstand. I happened to be one of the two people selected for one of the games. I found out later that these games made up the main floorshow.

I was one of two people singled out of the audience by the emcee. He pulled us onto center stage for a game. The other fellow, who was also a soldier, was selected first to perform on the stage. He was handed a broom that was to be held chest high and at full arms' length. His task was to high step across the floor over a series of milk bottles. When the emcee asked him if he thought he could do it without knocking over any of the milk bottles, he said he thought so. After he said that the emcee blindfolded him. The crowd really encouraged him but, to everyone's dismay, he knocked over several bottles.

When it came to my turn, the same procedure took place. My skill was to be matched against the skill of the other soldier. After I was blindfolded, I started across the stage. After a couple of high steps I heard the audience let out with a roar and started clapping. I thought they were cheering me on because so far I had not knocked over any of the bottles. I crossed the entire stage and never hit a bottle with my foot. I was mighty proud of my skill.

When I got to the other side my blindfold was removed and then I could see why the audience was laughing so hysterically. After I started my walk across the stage they removed all of the milk bottles. So here I was, high stepping across the stage, blindfolded, carrying a broom extended at arms' length. With the few drinks in me, I was having a ball and I had to laugh with them. I was duped...but it was all in good fun. The audience gave me a standing ovation when I took my seat.

By this time it was well past midnight and we felt that we should get back to camp. Joe hailed a cab and directed the driver to take us to his house. Upon arrival there, he got his car and drove us back to camp. Again we tried to give him some money, but he refused. That night cost him quite a few dollars.

What a day to remember. The last leg of my trip on the Atlantic Ocean entailed arrival in the good old USA, seeing an old friend and seeing New York City in all of its glory.

The next day, July 10th, brought me back to reality. The day proved to be a busy one. Regimentation was not over just yet. We were at Camp Kilmer for processing. After chow, the four of us went to the processing center where we were run through the rituals of getting our final physical and a series of interviews. There was a steady stream of Army personnel going through the separation process at the same time we were.

The next morning, July 11th, my buddies and I picked up our gear after breakfast and reported to the railhead to board the train to Ft. Meade. After a hot ride on the passenger train, we arrived at Ft. Meade near noon.

Ft. Meade was the place where soldiers were discharged, however, if anyone wanted to join the Reserves, arrangements were made to make this happen. I was given an opportunity to join the Active or Inactive Reserves.

An Army Major did a pretty good job to convince me that I should join the Inactive Reserves. I had already made up my mind before his rationale for joining the Reserves, so I did. The reason I joined was the fact that I truly felt that there was going to be another war within a few years, only this time it would be with Russia. If I were to reenter the Army to fight again, I wanted to protect my commission as a First Lieutenant and enter as an officer. So instead of being discharged, paperwork was processed to show that I was "Relieved From Active Duty" and transferred to the Inactive Reserves of the Army of the United States of America.

More interviews, more paperwork, and another physical. It certainly was much harder to get out of the Army than to get in. Because of some fluke, when I reported to the Finance Section to pick up my pay before leaving the center, I was told that my pay records had not reached there yet but that the money I had coming would be mailed to my home. I had not been paid since before I left Europe, so all the money I had was the money in my pocket. It was a good thing I didn't gamble it away on the ship when crossing the Atlantic.

Instead of an Honorable Discharge from the Army I was given a predated "Certificate of Service" showing that I honorably served in active Federal Service from June 9, 1945 to August 19, 1946, the date my terminal leave ended. Of course I was honorably discharged as a Staff Sergeant in Nachsheim, Germany when I accepted the commission as a Second Lieutenant.

I was always a proud soldier with any rank that I held. I was proud that I served my country faithfully and to the best of my ability in the time of war. I thanked God for the experience and even more, for returning home with all my faculties and a healthy body.

Through the processing, I said goodbye to my three friends, Lt. Lehr, Lt. Miller, and Capt. Truman, perhaps never to see them again. I was excited about returning home but sad about leaving my buddies.

The processing at Ft. Meade lasted the rest of the day. On Friday, July 12th, I received my orders to return home. I was given three days travel time and leave time before my pay terminated. This meant that August 19th would be my termination date for pay from the Army. The leave time was supposed to give a soldier enough time to return to his old job or to find a new one in civilian life.

I also received an official "script printed" appointment from the President of the United States granting me a Commission as a First Lieutenant. The President at that time was Harry S. Truman. I would hold this rank in an Inactive Reserve capacity until April 1, 1953 when my appointment would be terminated and I would then be granted an Honorable Discharge.

I purposely did not call Mary Lou because I knew that I would then call her as soon as I had definite information as to when I would be arriving Cincinnati.

After completing everything at Ft. Meade, my final station in the processing was to pick up my authorized travel orders for returning home.

Chapter 31

Epilogue

After leaving Ft. Meade, Maryland I boarded a bus to Washington, DC to Union Station where I was to take the train to Cincinnati, Ohio. I spent most of my money on a sleeping compartment because the train left at 6 p.m. and I wanted a good night's sleep before arriving in Cincinnati. I had called my Mom, Dad and Mary Lou (both collect calls) to tell them when I was arriving the next day. In all the anxiety I somehow lost my train reservation ticket. After franticly searching the train station in the areas where I had traveled I had no luck in finding it so I had to purchase another ticket. I thought I had enough money for coach fare to get home but was short a couple of dollars. By this time it was near boarding time. After telling the ticket agent about losing my ticket, he felt sorry for me and gave me the extra money out of his own pocket so I could go home. I couldn't thank him enough. Sitting up all night made the ride home long and boring. Worse yet I had no money left for food. What a way to return home.

The train was on time when I arrived at Union Terminal in Cincinnati. Mary Lou, Mom and Dad were there waiting for me with lots of hugs and kisses. What a great welcome I received after being overseas for almost two years.

After arriving at my parents' home I embraced my brother Bob, who I had not seen in well over two years. I changed into civilian clothes and never looked back. I avoided talking to anyone about my Army life and especially about my combat experiences. It made me uncomfortable to talk about the trauma I had been through, especially about being ambushed, captured and then my escape. That life was behind me and I wanted to look forward to a peaceful life in the years ahead of me.

In order for Mary Lou and I to get married I needed to find a job. Neither of us had much money because I gave most of my military pay to my parents. Within two weeks of searching for work I finally found a job selling life insurance, but I detested it. After a couple of months I quit my insurance job after finding another one more to my liking. On October 1, 1946, the Fisher Body Division of General Motors Corporation hired me. The Division was building a new metal fabricating plant south of Hamilton, Ohio. My position was that of a clerk working for the Tool & Die Superintendent.

Because of my pending marriage and the fact that my brother Bob and I needed to help our parents financially, I passed up using the GI Bill to go to college. I later realized how important a college education meant to my career. I then began attending evening college at the University of Cincinnati while working for the Fisher Body - Hamilton Plant. After several years, I received my degree in Personnel Administration.

On March 1, 1943 I was drafted into the Army. On April 1, 1953, ten years later, my military career officially ended. On this date I was relieved as a Reserve Officer and received my Honorable Discharge from the United States Army.

A year after being hired at the Hamilton Plant I transferred to the Employment Department as a clerk and a series of promotions over the next fourteen years took me to several supervisory positions in personnel work. I was eventually promoted to the executive position as Personnel Director for the plant on January 1, 1964.

After the war, rental apartments were difficult to find but Mary Lou and I were able to locate one in the Lindenwald area of Hamilton, Ohio. It was a second floor, three-room apartment where we shared the bath with the owners who lived downstairs. On February 15, 1947 Mary Louise Staarmann and I each left our parents' home and were married at St. Joseph's Catholic Church in Hamilton, Ohio.

Mary Lou and I bought our first home in May 1950. It was a four-room frame bungalow in Lindenwald. We remained there for six years and during that time the first of our two sons was born. Thomas D. Roberts was born on February 2, 1955.

In May 1956 we purchased a five-room brick ranch home in Fairfield, Ohio, just south of Hamilton, Ohio, where our second son, David J. Roberts, was born on March 22, 1960.

While living in Fairfield, Ohio I became quite active in community work. I served on many local boards, including the Chamber of Commerce, where I was president for two years; the library board and the hospital board in Hamilton, Ohio; the United Fund board; and chairman of fund drives for many years. I was also a member of the Board of Junior Achievement of Hamilton and Vicinity for many years and its Board Chairman for two years. I was the organizer of the Fairfield Safety Advisory Council for the city of Fairfield where I was its president for the first year.

On January 1, 1967, I was transferred to the Marion Plant of the Fisher Body Division of General Motors in Marion, Indiana as its Personnel Director. The plant had been having labor problems with its local union and needed help resolving the problems. Our family then moved to Marion, Indiana into a seven-room brick ranch home where our two sons began attending a new school the following September.

My tenure at the Marion Plant was not all that pleasant. However, with a lot of work and perseverance I accomplished my assignment and was rewarded on February 1, 1968 by being promoted and transferred to Fisher Body Division's General Offices in Warren, Michigan as its General Administrator of Salaried Personnel. This time when we moved we bought a new nine room, two-story colonial home in Bloomfield Hills, Michigan. Our family then had to become acquainted to another strange location and a new environment where our boys had to attend a different school again, which was difficult for them.

Three years later at General Offices, I was promoted to the position of Director of Personnel Services for the Division where my staff and I were responsible for coordinating most of the personnel activities for its thirty-two operating plants throughout the United States and Mexico. This job required a lot of business traveling. I retired from that position on November 1, 1986, after forty years of service with General Motors.

After retiring I did a lot of pleasure traveling. I traveled alone on most of my trips because Mary Lou did not like the way I traveled on the back roads and the "blue highways." I made two trips throughout many of the western states in a mini-van to visit the National Parks, National Monuments and other places of interest. The first trip I made was in April/May 1988 for six weeks. There was too much to see in just one trip that I had to schedule myself for another trip out west that took place in May/June 1992 for four weeks. Both trips were recorded on video so I could show my family.

Subsequent trips of this nature took me to the southern Unites States and another trip to the eastern United States visiting the various states and many places of interest, which were historical and educational as well.

In the early spring of 1987, at the urging of my two sons, Tom and Dave, I began writing my autobiography. In my research about the "war years," I learned that since 1947 my former Army Division, the 106th Infantry Division had been organized as an Association for all veterans who once served with the Division. I joined the Association that year and attended my first national reunion in Schaumburg, Illinois in September 1989. This is where I met my Army buddy and good friend John Schaffner who I served with in Battery "A," 589th Field Artillery Battalion. We had lost contact with each other, which so many soldiers do after the war, and we became reacquainted at that reunion. We renewed our bond of friendship, which continues to prevail.

During our marriage, Mary Lou and I did take several trips to her liking, which included three cruises, one to the Caribbean, another to Alaska and finally through the Panama Canal. The last trip we took together as an entire family was a two-week trip to Hawaii in 1974. After our Alaskan cruise, I was able to say that I had fulfilled my goal to visit all fifty of the United States in my lifetime.

Many wonderful things happened in my life since I retired. I was proud to see both of our sons, Tom and Dave, go to college and receive their masters degrees and enter excellent careers for themselves. Other significant memorable occasions were the marriage of both Tom and Dave. Tom married Julie Bauer on April 29, 1978. They have three children: Matthew, Michael and Christina. David married Susan Dryden on April 22, 1989 and they have two children, Jonathan and Cecilia.

I returned to Europe on two occasions. The first trip was in September 1994 when I took a military tour with several veterans of the 106th Infantry Division Association to the Ardennes to find the various places we fought during the Battle of the Bulge. I desperately tried to find where I was ambushed but was not able to find it. I did, however, travel the same road. I also tried to find the gravesite of my good friend Carl Himberg who was killed in an ambush and now buried in Henri Chapelle Military Cemetery near Liege, Belgium. I also failed in that attempt and felt very bad about it. I did not return to the United States with the tour group. I remained in Europe for several weeks touring Germany, Austria, Switzerland and Italy by train with stops at major cities to see the sights. I rented a car in Vienna, Austria and drove all over the country, visiting Salzburg, Kirchdorf and Linz, where I was stationed while serving as a Military Government officer.

In May 1997, Mary Lou and I, along with our immediate family, held a gala reception and dinner for our family, relatives and friends for about 200 people to celebrate our 50th wedding anniversary at a local hotel. It was a celebration never to be forgotten.

In May 1999, I again returned to Germany a second time and this time for the purpose of visiting the exact spot where I was ambushed and captured, and to visit the gravesite of my friend Carl Himberg. I was confident that I would find the spot where I was ambushed because Hans Wijers from The Netherlands would escort me there.

This was made possible when Hans Wijers, a historian and author of several books about WWII and the Battle of the Bulge, was going through the German War Archives in Koblenz, Germany where he found a photograph of a disabled weapons carrier sitting in a ditch. Seeing it was an American vehicle, he sent the photograph to John Kline, editor of *The Cub* magazine of the 106th Infantry Division Association. Mr. Kline could not identify the vehicle so he published it in *The Cub* magazine for the quarterly issue in the fall of 1995 to see if any of the Association members could identify the vehicle.

When I saw the picture of the disabled weapons carrier in the magazine I was shocked. I couldn't believe it! I was looking at the second vehicle in the two-vehicle convoy that I was in when the Germans ambushed us on the way to our forward observation post in Roth, Germany on the morning of December 16, 1944. I immediately wrote Mr. Kline a letter telling him of the events leading up to the ambush and why the weapons carrier was sitting in the ditch. A German news photographer had taken the photograph shortly after our group was ambushed.

John Kline published my detailed letter in *The Cub* in the 1996 spring edition and put me in contact with Hans Wijers. Using the photograph of the weapons carrier and its background in the picture, along with the detailed chapters about the ambush from my autobiography that I sent to him, Mr. Wijers went to the area I described and was able to pinpoint the exact spot of the ambush. Hans took pictures of the ambush site and sent them to me telling me that if I should ever return to Germany, he would personally escort me to the spot where I was ambushed. Because of this uncanny story, Mr. Kline also put my letter on his web site under the title of "Ambush."

The opportunity to return to the Ardennes came about in May 1999 when I returned to Germany with a group of 106th Infantry Division Veterans organized by John Kline. That is when Hans Wijers drove from The Netherlands to Prum, Germany where on May 18, 1999 he met me at the small hotel where I was staying and drove me to the exact spot, which I immediately recognized. This visit was a triumph and one of great emotion for me.

Also, the trip to Europe in 1999 afforded me the opportunity to visit the grave site of Carl Himberg in Henri Chapelle Military Cemetery where I was personally escorted to his grave site by several of my Belgian friends, whom I had met in 1994 on my first trip to Europe. Since 1994 these friends have maintained his gravesite with an American flag and flowers on special occasions.

At the end of the May 1999 tour, I remained overseas in Europe to fly from Frankfurt, Germany to London, England for a week's tour and then a train ride under the English Channel to

Paris, France for an additional week's tour before flying home from Paris. It was a trip I will never forget.

As a result of my "Ambush" story appearing on John Kline's web site I have had veterans as well as other people contact me about my story. Among those making a contact were members of Carl Himberg's family. I was able to tell them of my association with Carl as an Army buddy and how he was killed in action. This was valuable information they were not able to get from the Department of the Army.

Laura Walker Slinkard, daughter of Captain John T. Walker, who saved my life and the lives of my comrades on the first day of the Battle of the Bulge by engineering our escape from the village of Weckerath, also contacted me. I was able to tell Laura about my experiences with her father, who commanded Troop "C" of the 14th Cavalry, as well as to put her in contact with the 14th Cavalry Association.

In recent years I have been giving many talks to tell my "Ambush" story in order to pass along to succeeding generations just one story of the kind of sacrifices that many men and women made during WWII in both theaters of operation in order for the United States of America to remain free. My story is only one of millions of stories. Not many veterans of WWII are still alive. As of this writing there are only 4 million alive of the 11 million veterans of WWII and we are dying at the rate of 1,500 each day. One of these days we will all be gone. I seize every opportunity to tell my story for the history records, including this book.

In my later years of life my health has been reasonably good except for losing my left kidney due to cancer in May 2001. I have had bladder cancer four times and successfully beat the odds by getting rid of the cancer through surgery and a form of chemotherapy treatments. Then in June 2002, I suffered a heart attack and had angioplasty with a stent packed in my right artery. I now consider myself in good health through proper medication, restricted diet and plenty of exercise.

I have attended most all of the national reunions of the 106th Infantry Division since 1989 and was elected to the board of directors in the 2000. In 2001, I was elected to 2nd Vice President and in 2002 to 1st Vice President. The good Lord willing, I should be able to serve a years term as its president beginning in September 2003.

God has been good to me. I have enjoyed my life to the fullest and look forward to spending many of my remaining years with my family and friends, who mean so much to me.

This may be the end of my book but not the end of memories which will prevail for many years by those who remember me and those who read of my exploits and realize that John M. "Jack" Roberts had principle and was a devoted man to his religion, family, friends, his job and to his country.

God bless you for reading my book and may God Bless America.

Bob Roberts, Jack Roberts and Grace Roberts (Dad and Mom)
June 1944

Grace Roberts
Harrison Ave
March 25, 1943

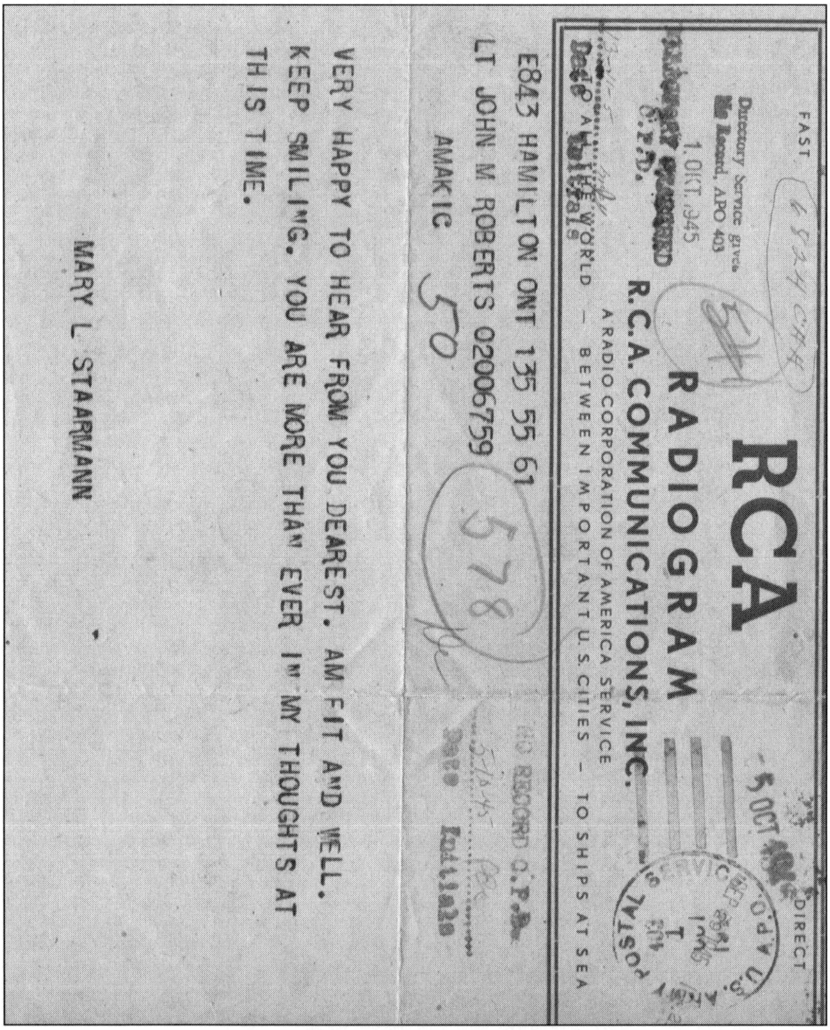

FAST

Directory Service gives No Record, APO 403

1 OKT 1945

C.P.D.

Date

RCA

RADIOGRAM

R.C.A. COMMUNICATIONS, INC.

A RADIO CORPORATION OF AMERICA SERVICE

TO ALL THE WORLD — BETWEEN IMPORTANT U.S. CITIES — TO SHIPS AT SEA

DIRECT

NO RECORD C.P.D.

Date Initials

E843 HAMILTON ONT 135 55 61

LT JOHN M ROBERTS 02006759

AMAKIC

VERY HAPPY TO HEAR FROM YOU DEAREST. AM FIT AND WELL.
KEEP SMILING. YOU ARE MORE THAN EVER IN MY THOUGHTS AT
THIS TIME.

MARY L STAARMANN

Mary Lou Staarman and Jack Roberts
August 1944

F 3/C Robert Roberts and Cpl. Jack Roberts
B&O Station, Hamilton, Ohio
September 5, 1943

Carl Himberg, Jack Roberts, and Gene Epperson
Sunday April 30, 1944

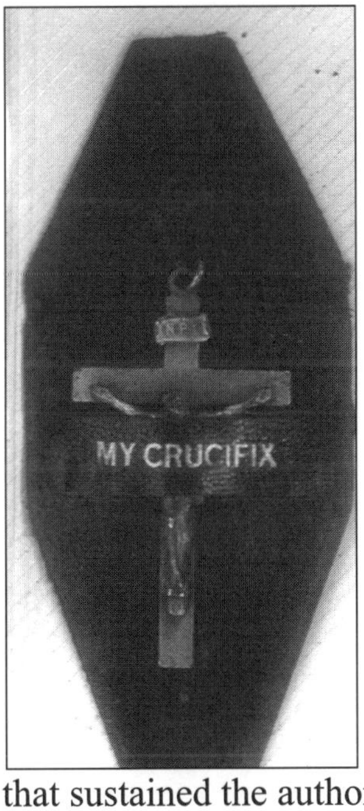

This is the crucifix that sustained the author's faith throughout the war. When the Germans captured and searched Jack, all of his personal belongings were removed except this crucifix, which they failed to find in his pocket.

HAMILTON JOURNAL AND DAILY NEWS
FRIDAY, JUNE 29, 1945

TWO HAMILTONIANS WIN BATTLEFIELD COMMISSIONS

Wm. C. Maxwell Now Lieutenant

LIEUTENANT MAXWELL

Two men from Hamilton, William C. Maxwell and John M. Roberts, who have been in the army since March, 1943, were given battlefield commissions this month within one day of each other. Each holds the rank of second lieutenant in the army of the United States.

Since their induction, the army careers of these two have run parallel until the last few months. They received their first training at Jackson, S. C., and later were sent to Camp Atterbury, Ind.

Lieutenant Rank Given To Roberts

LIEUTENANT ROBERTS

Lieutenant Maxwell and Lieutenant Roberts departed for England in October, 1944. Lieutenant Maxwell was sent into Belgium and later Germany, while Lieutenant Roberts remained in France a short time and then was sent to Germany.

Both men participated in the battle of the Ardennes forest at St. Vith in December, 1944. Lieutenant Roberts also took part in the battle of the Belgian bulge. During this battle, he had the experience of being captured and held prisoner for about a week until he made his escape.

According to the latest information received by their parents, Lieutenant Maxwell is serving with the Fifteenth army at Heilbraun, Germany, and Lieutenant Roberts is with the First army in Mayan, Germany. Lieutenant Roberts recently told his parents that he expects to remain in Europe for occupational duty.

Lieutenant Maxwell is the son of Mr. and Mrs. Allen C. Maxwell, 601 Ross avenue. During his five months of combat participation, he earned four battle stars. He was a technical sergeant before he was commissioned June 11.

A staff sergeant before he was commissioned June 10, Lieutenant Roberts is the son of Mr. and Mrs. Robert Roberts, 408 Harrison avenue. He was employed by the Keiser Clothing company before his induction and holds three battle stars. He has a brother, Robert, machinist's mate second class, is with the navy in the South Pacific.

Lt. Jack Roberts
Arrival home from Army
Harrison Ave.
July 13, 1946